Praise for *Pearl Harbor Christmas*

"[Weintraub] captures what it was like to live through one of the most infamous holiday seasons in American history."
—*Portland Book Review*

"A fascinating and compelling look at the events immediately following the 'Day of Infamy'"—*Deseret News*

"[An] exceptional piece of historical reporting"
—King Features Syndicate

"Authoritative... swift-moving"—*Richmond Times-Dispatch*

"Rich anecdotal material... of what went on behind the scenes."
—*Norfolk Virginian-Pilot*

"A quick and smooth read"—*Milwaukee Shepherd-Express*

"[A] lively account"—*Toronto Globe & Mail*

"[A] 'fly-on-the-wall' eye for fascinating detail."
—*Sunday Missoulian*

"Weintraub deftly weaves the pivotal, the noteworthy, and the curious."—*America in WWII*

"Enlightening"—*Military Review*

"Dazzling"—*Publishers Weekly*

"Vivid"—*Kirkus Reviews*

"Stirring"—*Library Journal*

"Absorbing"—*Booklist*

PEARL HARBOR CHRISTMAS

A World at War, December 1941

Stanley Weintraub

Da Capo Press
A Member of the Perseus Books Group

Editorial production by *Marra*thon Production Services, www.marrathon.net

DESIGN BY JANE RAESE
Text set in 12-point Adobe Caslon Pro

Library of Congress Cataloging-in-Publication Data is available for this book.
ISBN 978-0-306-82061-8 (hardcover)
ISBN 978-0-306-82062-5 (e-book)
ISBN 978-0-306-82153-0 (paperback)

First Da Capo Press edition 2011
First Da Capo Press paperback edition 2012

Published by Da Capo Press
A Member of the Perseus Books Group
www.dacapopress.com

Da Capo Press books are available at special discounts for bulk purchases in the U.S. by corporations, institutions, and other organizations. For more information, please contact the Special Markets Department at the Perseus Books Group, 2300 Chestnut Street, Suite 200, Philadelphia, PA 19103, or call (800) 810-4145, ext. 5000, or e-mail special.markets@perseusbooks.com.

10 9 8 7 6 5 4 3 2

FOR RODELLE

Contents

Prelude

IN TOKYO ON THE MORNING of December 21, 1941, the *Asahi Shimbun* published on its front page the first photo received of the attack on Pearl Harbor. It had been flown in by a dive bomber from the strike force returning to the Home Islands. Approaching Hawaii on its last leg from Washington was an investigating commission appointed by President Franklin D. Roosevelt and chaired by Supreme Court Justice Owen Roberts. It would be the first of many hearings on the worst military catastrophe in American history. As its plane approached Oahu, smoke, although no longer in billowing black clouds, rose from the wreckages in the harbor area. At aircraft height the upturned hulls of the capsized *Oklahoma* and *Utah* resembled beached whales.

Justice Roberts would convene his inquiry the next day, as across the nation the President expected Prime Minister Winston Churchill for dinner at the White House. Pearl Harbor had made them open wartime allies. One small logistic problem intervened, however. Late that morning the Prime Minister was still at sea. The battleship *Duke of York* was plowing through winter winds and heavy swells as it approached Chesapeake Bay. By radio, assuming a calmer Atlantic, Churchill had accepted Roosevelt's invitation. On docking in the upper Chesapeake, it would be only a 120-mile drive to Washington. Yet, increasingly anxious

Front page of the December 21, 1941, morning edition of *Asahi Shimbun* with the first picture of the Pearl Harbor attack, showing bombed Hickam Field by Japanese planes. *Courtesy* Asahi Shimbun

U.S. battleships under air attack at Pearl Harbor, as photographed by a Japanese pilot. *U.S. Navy*

at the warship's slow progress, the PM was, as his personal physician, Sir Charles Wilson,* recalled, "like a child in his impatience to meet the President. He spoke as if every minute counted. It was absurd to waste time. He must fly."

Radioing his ambassador, the Earl of Halifax, the PM requested help. "Impossible to reach Mouth Potomac before 6:30 P.M. which would be too late. . . . I should like to come by airplane to [a] Washington airfield reaching you in time for dinner." Halifax telephoned the White House, which ordered a squat twin-engine Lockheed Lodestar to Hampton Roads, where the battleship would dock. Churchill, his close adviser Lord Beaverbrook (proprietor of the *Evening Standard* and Minister of Supply), and several aides boarded the aircraft for the forty-five minute flight up the Potomac. The others awaited a special train to Washington sent by the Baltimore & Ohio Railroad, which would bring them to the capital by midnight.

Early winter darkness had fallen. Emerging from years of blackouts—ships also traveled without running lights to evade German submarines—the party aboard the transport plane was amazed to see the spectacle below. Few Americans anywhere had yet to follow recent blackout instructions. It was Christmas.

The Anacostia Flats Naval Air Station was across the Potomac from the new National Airport. Awaiting at the tarmac was a long, black limousine that the Treasury Department had confiscated from Al Capone. The Chicago gangster was now in prison. Roosevelt had been sitting in the car, waiting. "Please on no account come out to meet me," Churchill had radioed. As the aircraft taxied to a stop and Churchill emerged, gripping a walking stick to which what the English called an electric torch was attached, for use in navigating blackouts, the President was lifted out and was standing, leaning against the limo, propped by his

---

*Later he became Lord Moran.

locked leg braces and a cane. "I grasped his strong hand with comfort and pleasure," Churchill recalled.

———— ∞∞∞ ————

WHEN RADIO REPORTS that Hawaii had been attacked reached England, Churchill was at his official residence, Chequers, at dinner with Lend-Lease administrator W. Averell Harriman and Ambassador John G. Winant. "I do not pretend to have measured accurately the martial might of Japan," the PM wrote in his memoirs, "but at this very moment I knew the United States was in the war, up to the neck and in to the death. So we had won after all!" Curiously, Adolf Hitler was equally delighted about his prospects once Pearl Harbor had given him Japan as a partner. "We can't lose the war at all," he thought. "We now have an ally which has never been conquered in 3,000 years."

After the news of Pearl Harbor, Churchill claimed to have "slept the sleep of the saved and thankful." Actually, he stayed up until three talking with Winant about what to do next, and he determined to go to Washington. Seven months earlier, on May 3, feeling increasingly isolated and with German submarines strangling British lifelines worldwide, he had desperately cabled Roosevelt pleading for immediate American entry into the war—a plea he had made even earlier, in June 1940, as France surrendered to Hitler. In neither case could the President intervene overtly. Americans were unready, and Congress would have resisted. Roosevelt had to inch his way toward rescue, as he did symbolically when Britain's new envoy arrived in January 1941.

———— ∞∞∞ ————

GREETING CHURCHILL PERSONALLY remained an unusual honor for a head of government, especially when proffered by a long-incapacitated president, who had done so only once before—and then, too, to emphasize his solidarity with Britain. Ambassador Halifax, once of the influential appeasement fraternity in England, had crossed the Atlantic on the battleship *George V* and was greeted in Chesapeake Bay, six miles from Annapolis, by the presidential yacht *Potomac,* with Roosevelt aboard. Viscount Halifax then traveled into Washington with FDR. It was a precedent-shattering gesture, and Halifax was ever afterward "Edward" to Roosevelt.

What the public did not know was that the pair, however effective their relationship would be, was a brotherhood of the disabled. Roosevelt had lost the use of his legs to polio in 1921, and the tall, lean Edward Wood, then heir to his father's title, had been born with a withered left arm without a hand.

"Now that we are as you say 'in the same boat' wouldn't it be wise for us," Churchill had cabled on December 9, "to have another conference?" They had met at sea, on Placentia Bay off Newfoundland in early August, initiating what would become after Pearl Harbor a formal military alliance. "We could review," Churchill now suggested, "the whole war plan in the light of reality and new facts, as well as production and distribution. I feel that all these matters . . . can best be settled on the highest executive level." He could leave "in a day or two" by warship and bring with him "necessary staffs." In a draft of his war memoirs the PM wrote, then expunged, "I thought of staying in the British Embassy, as I did not know how stiff our discussions might be."

Startled, Roosevelt would have opted for more time to see how war mobilization was going and the situation in the Pacific was "more clarified." He planned to respond that way in a draft he never sent. In a second response, on December 10, also unsent, he wrote that a meeting would be "more useful a few weeks hence than immediately. However I will wholeheartedly and gladly accept your opinion on timing." The President's advisers realized that the British would come with carefully drafted proposals and a substantial wish list of war materiel before the White House could scramble to create its own strategies and review its production goals. Also there was concern over the hazards to the top levels of British government. The North Atlantic was a shooting gallery for German subs, and the Luftwaffe flew reconnaissance from French and Norwegian bases.

The third presidential reply, actually sent later that day, began, "Delighted to have you here at White House. . . . My one reservation is great person[al] risk to you—believe this should be given most careful consideration for the Empire needs you at the helm and we need you there too." Having postponed sailing while keeping a convoy at the ready, Churchill notified those who were to travel with him and packed his bags.

His formal invitation to stay at the White House came via Lord Halifax while Churchill was at sea. Although he had invited himself, a strong hint to do so had come from the President in a telegram announcing Congress's formal declaration of war on Japan on December 8. "Today," Roosevelt had written in the naval metaphors both leaders shared, "all of us are in the same boat with you and the people of the Empire and it is a ship which will not and cannot be sunk." The "same boat" image was echoed in Churchill's cable to Washington.

Ambassador Winant in London telegraphed Harry Hopkins at the White House via Secretary of State Cordell Hull (the proper protocol): "Our friend asked me if the house was large enough to permit him to have with him a secretary and his valet." The PM (soon "the Prime" to the President's staff) had accepted while at sea, enlarging his personal entourage at the White House to his confidant "Max" Beaverbrook, John Martin (Churchill's principal secretary), two security men, and the PM's valet. The rest of the party, including Averell Harriman, were to be housed nearby at the Mayflower Hotel on Pennsylvania Avenue rather than at the more distant British Embassy.

"At first," Roy Jenkins, a later Cabinet minister, has written, "Churchill had intended to stay only about a week, but as his visit lengthened, he became near to a real-life version of *The Man Who Came to Dinner*." In the hit comedy of 1939–40 by George S. Kaufman and Moss Hart, the radio personality Sheridan Whiteside, mellifluous and charming at the microphone, having apparently broken his leg on departing the home of a socially prominent Washington couple, is rushed back indoors to heal in a wheelchair, becoming an insufferable long-term guest.

The worldwide disasters of the weekend of Pearl Harbor made it urgent for the Prime Minister as well as the President to pool global strategies. "As soon as I awoke" the morning after, Churchill claimed, "I decided to go over at once to see Roosevelt." He feared that the immediate impact of Pearl Harbor would be a retreat into an "America-comes-first" attitude in Washington, withholding aid to Britain and Russia while concentrating resources to strike back at Japan. In solidarity with Japan, Adolf Hitler would make that "Europe last" likelihood moot by declaring war on the United States, but isolationists who had inveighed against involvement in European wars were still influential in Congress, and the attacks on the United States had come in the Pacific. Roosevelt's cordial invitation to the White House put a new slant on everything.

Before the PM embarked on December 12, he engaged in strategy sessions with his advisers, who recommended continuing the careful language they had employed with America before the new dimension to the war. Sir Alan Brooke, the new chief of the imperial general staff, recalled that Churchill turned to one in the cautious circle "*with a wicked leer in his eye*" and said, "Oh!

7

That is the way we talked to her while we were wooing her; now that she is in the harem we talk to her quite differently!"

That open cynicism would be dispensed with in Washington. The Japanese were winning everywhere on the Pacific Rim. Across the Atlantic, embattled Britain, supplied largely by sea, was losing as many freighters to U-boats as were being built to replace the sinkings. Malaya was being overrun, and its 220-square mile island appendage, Singapore, was unlikely to hold out. Hong Kong had been invaded and had no hope of survival; Wake Island had been attacked and Guam quickly occupied; and in the Philippines the Japanese were already on Luzon and bombing Manila. Australia seemed threatened, and Hawaiians worried that, with the navy and air forces on Oahu decimated, the Japanese might return.

After much politics-as-usual debate about the appropriate age for draft registration, Congress on December 19 had timidly settled on twenty for induction and eighteen for registration. On both the Atlantic and Pacific coasts, the services had hurriedly set anti-aircraft guns on the roofs of buildings and alongside docks. Some weapons were obsolete, others wooden fakes, there to instill spurious confidence. Sentries, often bearing 1918-vintage rifles, were posted at railway stations and armaments factories. Although the only interloper likely over the American skies at Christmas was likely to be Santa Claus with his sleigh and reindeer, a twenty-four-hour sky watch in the Northeast was ordered for the holidays by Brigadier General John C. MacDonnell, air-raid warning chief for 43,000 volunteer civilian observers. "Experience in war," he declared, "has taught that advantage is taken of relaxation in vigilance to strike when and where the blow is least expected." Lights remained on almost everywhere.

Anxiety on the Pacific coast about Japanese air raids, however absurd, had already panicked San Francisco, thanks to the paranoia of Fourth Army commander Lieutenant General John

DeWitt at Fort Ord. Every Japanese fisherman and vegetable farmer along the coast was suspected of covertly warning nonexistent enemy aircraft, and the hysteria resulted in the relocation of the New Year's Day Rose Bowl extravaganza from California to somnolent Durham, North Carolina, where Duke University would play Oregon State.

On war maps in the press, limited to much less than the actual facts, a dismal Christmas loomed, but it did not appear that way in shop windows across America. Enhanced by holiday lights, the street lamps and store fronts glittered, and a plethora of merchandise long vanished from high streets in Britain awaited shoppers now benefiting from jobs created by proliferating war contracts and a burgeoning army and navy. Christmas trees were plentiful, seldom priced at more than a dollar or two, and in the traditional holiday spectacle at Radio City Music Hall in New York, the star-spangled Rockettes, in mechanical unison, high-stepped away any war gloom. In newspapers across the nation the Japanese were thwarted in the *Terry and the Pirates* comic strip, and in film Gary Cooper as Sergeant York was defeating the Germans single-handedly in the earlier world war.

The hit book for Christmas giving, at a hefty $2.50, was Edna Ferber's Reconstruction-era romance *Saratoga Trunk*. For the same price, war turned up distantly yet bombastically in a two-disc set of Tchaikovsky's *1812 Overture,* performed by Artur Rodzinski and the Cleveland Orchestra. In New York gift crates of oranges and grapefruit from Florida were $2.79 at Bloomingdale's. A new Ford or Chevrolet, both soon to be unobtainable, cost $900. Hattie Carnegie's designer dresses began at $15. The upscale Rogers Peet menswear store offered suits and topcoats from a steep $38. (At recruiting stations nationwide, the army was offering smart khaki garb at no cost whatever to enlistees.) Henri Bendel featured silk stockings at $1.25 a pair; stockings in the current wonder weave, *nylon,* sold for $1.65. By the following

Christmas nylons would be almost unobtainable. The fabric would be the stuff of parachutes.

Among the long-prepared Christmas toy glut, shops across America advertised a remote-control bombing plane at $1.98, which ran along a suspended wire to attack a battleship. The Japanese high seas *Kido Butai* had not needed suspended wires at Pearl Harbor, nor in the Philippines, Malaya, or Hong Kong. The Royal Navy's principal warships on the Pacific Rim were at the bottom of the Gulf of Siam, and the depleted Pacific Fleet, with seven battleships sunk or disabled at their anchorages, had only two destroyers available to patrol the long coastline between Vancouver and San Diego. As Churchill would put it, "Over all this vast expanse of waters Japan was supreme, and we everywhere [were] weak and naked."

On the other side of the continent, thoroughly open to attacks if there were to be any, the Prime Minister, having embarked from the River Clyde in Scotland on December 14, was already in the mid-Atlantic on the new battleship *Duke of York* amid violent, frigid gales. Aware from his office of her husband's falling behind schedule, Clementine Churchill cabled him from London on December 19: "You have been gone a week & all the news of you is of heavy seas delaying your progress—plans to change into planes at Bermuda, so as to arrive in time, & then those plans cancelled. . . . May God keep you and inspire you to make good plans with the President. It is a horrible World at present. Europe overrun by the Nazi hogs, & the Far East by yellow Japanese lice. I am spending Christmas here . . . & going to Chequers on Saturday the 27th."

In Washington the American brass worried even before Churchill departed about having the PM at Roosevelt's elbow, where, despite Britain's weak hand getting even weaker, he could employ his glib persuasiveness and imperial visions.

En Route

CHURCHILL AND HIS STAFF had taken the overnight train from London to Greenock on the Clyde. They reached the *Duke of York* on the morning of December 13, three days after its sister ship, *Prince of Wales,* and heavy cruiser *Repulse,* had been sunk by Japanese torpedo bombers off Malaya. Vice Admiral Sir Tom Phillips had rushed both warships north toward the enemy invasion fleet without any air cover. The shock and humiliation were great, and the strategic loss was irreversible. Still, the Prime Minister could claim confidence that American involvement—and American industrial potential—would inevitably reverse the Axis tide.

By radio aboard—and twenty-seven code clerks working round the clock—the PM kept in touch with events. The Germans were deep into Russia but slowed almost to stalemate by stiff resistance and heavy snow. Blaming faltering commanders for the crisis, Berlin radio reported, Adolf Hitler had assumed supreme command of the *Wehrmacht.* The Japanese were already exceeding their own expectations in Malaya and the Philippines and intent on driving the Dutch from the oil fields of Borneo. Hong Kong's invaders, ordered to take mainland Kowloon and the island in ten days, were experiencing unexpected resistance, but there were no escape routes. While the sandbagged and surrounded Repulse Bay Hotel on the beautiful eastern shore, packed with frightened guests and refugees and defended by grimy, nearly sleepless, soldiers, was being shelled, an English lady who had paid a steep £10 a day for her stay complained loudly, "What are all those Chinese people doing here?"

From the start the *Duke of York* and its passengers and crew endured a rough crossing. Swept by gales and high seas, the splashed decks were off limits for the first three days. Over the protestations of Dr. Wilson, Churchill dosed himself below with Mothersills Seasick Remedy ("Stops travel nausea on your vacation trips," the label advertised), and he began offering seasick stories to his queasy companions. At the dining table, when the PM chatted gaily about the special-purpose buckets he had once seen on the bridge of a destroyer, Sir John Dill made a queasy exit. There was no stopping the former First Lord of the Admiralty, who told about the desperate passenger on an ocean liner who was rushing to the nearest rail when a steward warned, "But sir, you can't be sick here!"

"Oh, can't I?" said the passenger as he kept going.

Reaching the Azores without incident, the Churchill party could transmit business there safely by radio. A hundred miles farther out, plowing ahead of buffeted light escort vessels, which were forced to turn back, the battleship maintained outgoing radio silence, but events did not make that easy for the Prime Minister. "Our very large deciphering staff," he recalled, "could of course receive by wireless [radio] a great deal of business. To a limited extent we could reply. When fresh escorts joined us from the Azores they could take in by daylight Morse signals from us in code, and then, dropping off a hundred miles or so, could transmit them without revealing our position. Still, there was a sense of radio claustrophobia. . . ."

IN WASHINGTON radiograms brought in increasingly bad news. In the central Pacific a handful of marines and marine pilots had held off the Japanese at isolated Wake Island after repelling a landing on the eleventh, but after another attempt, their overwhelmed remnants were buckling. The nation had been electrified by a brash radiogram from Wake, "Send us more Japs!"—but it was at best an imaginative misreading of a much more gloomy message. Although the isolated garrison was doomed, it had accomplished a feat never repeated during the war—fending off an amphibious force with coastal guns.

In the doomed Philippines on the twenty-second, General Douglas MacArthur, having boasted before Pearl Harbor that he was ready to meet any Japanese thrust, sat in his headquarters in an historic old fortress in Manila near his hotel penthouse flat as alarming reports came in about troop withdrawals. Forty-three thousand Japanese began swarming ashore at Lingayen Gulf in central Luzon, although MacArthur prepared defiant communiqués claiming otherwise.

Like the British in Malaya withdrawing southward on the four hundred-mile-long Kra Peninsula toward theoretically invulnerable Singapore, protected by the natural moat of the Strait of Johore, MacArthur's ground forces were unprepared, underequipped, and quickly shorn of air and naval support. American subs off the Philippines had attacked enemy transports, but their poorly designed torpedo fuses did not work. Much of the air force on Luzon had been destroyed on the ground, although MacArthur had received ample warning about likely attacks. But for sporadic air raids met with futile anti-aircraft weapons geared in altitude settings for an earlier war, Manila was quiet. Its population, with nowhere to go, was passive and anxious. Preparing to leave for the tadpole-shaped "rock" of Corregidor in Manila Bay, considered as impregnable as Singapore, the general drew up a proclamation, its release still withheld, declaring Manila an open city. By the laws of war ignored by the Japanese elsewhere, the declaration meant that by Christmas the city would be undefended and thus exempt—on paper—from bombardment.

MacArthur then sent for Lieutenant Colonel Sid Huff, a retired naval officer who had become a personal assistant commissioned on the general's behalf. "Sid," said MacArthur, "I've forgotten to buy Jean a Christmas present." Whatever would be purchased would be less than useless on Corregidor, but Huff was to think of something for Mrs. MacArthur. Philippine money would also be useless, and the general had plenty of it to lavish on Manila shops. Loyally, Huff went off to places he knew Jean patronized and would know her size (twelve), returning with boxes of dresses and lingerie bound with Christmas ribbons. MacArthur crossed the street from venerable, walled Intramuros in Calle Victoria, took the elevator to his Manila Hotel penthouse flat on the sixth floor—with seven bedrooms and a state dining room and a ten thousand–volume military history library built for him in 1935. He advised Jean to open the gifts right away. Christmas Eve might be too late.

War tension was lost on little Arthur IV, who would celebrate his fourth birthday in a tunnel on Corregidor in February. He had a gaily decorated Christmas tree in the family penthouse, and his presents were in a closet, never to be stacked under the tree on Christmas Eve after his bedtime. That evening his parents announced it was the day before Christmas, which it wasn't, and extricated his presents for unwrapping. One was a tricycle, which he pedaled happily round the spacious flat and its balconies while his mother opened her own gifts with pretended joy. She examined each, holding the contents one at a time to admire. "Sir Boss, they are beautiful," she said as she began rewrapping them for departure. "Thank you so much." Mark Twain's fictional Connecticut Yankee who dominated King Arthur's court was addressed as "Sir Boss," and Jean had adopted it.

KEEPING BUSY AT SEA, Churchill dictated position papers on "The Atlantic Front" and "The Pacific Front" to offer the President, suggesting the dispatch of American troops to Northern Ireland and bomber squadrons to Scotland in order to relieve British forces for action. Overestimating the American pace of preparedness, he envisaged beginning the liberation of Europe little more than a year later—the subject of a third paper, "The Campaign of 1943." In the postwar publication of his papers, silently edited, he omitted the paper on the Pacific front, giving that title to a fourth, originally "Notes on the Pacific." He may have felt embarrassed about the hopes he had held for Singapore, expected to hold the Japanese back for six months until rescue. What he did print, however, was equally complacent, expecting that by May 1942, only five months distant, the Allies could mass a formidable battle fleet in the Pacific, bolstered by aircraft carriers yet to be built and "improvised carriers" converted from existing merchantmen and warships. The Royal Navy had begun employing "escort carriers" for convoy duty, and Roosevelt would initiate a program to refit freighters under construction as small carriers, then order escort carriers designed as such. (Of 151 American carriers constructed during the war, 122 would be escort size. Only 5 would be lost to enemy action.)

Ever the optimist, Churchill saw the military resources of Japan, dependent on what could be exploited from occupied territories that he expected the allies to retrieve, as a "wasting factor" leading to inevitable defeat. His two service chiefs, Admiral Sir Dudley Pound and Air Chief Marshal Sir Charles Portal, concurred. Abetted, apparently, by Portal, the PM promoted deploying air power that did not yet exist from locations that also did not exist for massive air assaults on Japan itself to retard further "overseas adventures" and bring the war directly to the Japanese islands. "The burning of Japanese cities by incendiary bombs," he wrote in a paragraph he did not reprint postwar, "will bring home in a most effective manner to the people of Japan the dangers of the course to which they have committed themselves." That would indeed happen, three years later, but not because American planners and aircraft engineers had read the PM's papers.

Field Marshal Sir John Dill, who had been replaced at the War Office by Brooke, was expected to remain in Washington as liaison. Although Churchill had sniffed about him as "Dilly-Dally," he had the backbone to disagree with the Prime Minister and took some risky decisions for which the PM would take postwar credit. Pushing Dill out of the way so that Churchill could run the war through personal surrogates proved inadvertently to be one of the Prime Minister's best appointments. Remembered for his observation, "It takes a lot of moral courage not to be afraid of being thought afraid," Dill became an intimate of American chief of staff General George Marshall, and he was so highly regarded throughout the war that on his death late in 1944 he was buried, with Congressional approval, at Arlington.

After FDR had sent Churchill a memorandum suggesting a "Joint Staff Conference" with their American counterparts "as to how we are going to fight the war together," the PM convened his own military advisers aboard on December 18, along with the Minister of Supply, Lord Beaverbrook. Canadian-born William Maxwell Aitken, a controversial Hearst-like newspaper baron who owned the *Daily and Sunday Express* and the *Evening Standard* and promoted appeasement during the tawdry Thirties, had become a relentless foe of Hitlerism once war erupted. Having only produced newsprint, he had become the tireless and inventive war production czar in Churchill's ministry.

Further staff meetings were called as the *Duke of York* struggled in turbulent waters. In his cabin on the bridge, Churchill sipped brandy, took naps, and read two books he had brought along—a novel about Napoleon and Josephine, and a World War I sea story by C. S. Forester, author of the Hornblower series the PM loved. He watched a movie every evening, with his favorite *Blood and Sand,* a bullfighting epic starring Rita Hayworth and Clark Gable—who, at forty-one, would soon be a gunner in action on a B-17. Churchill also enjoyed *The Sea Hawk*, with Errol Flynn and Claude Rains, in which Queen Elizabeth (Flora Robson), desiring to spare the purses of her subjects, hesitates to fund ships to defend England against the Spanish Armada. "You see," Churchill told Harriman as the film wound down, "The British have always been the biggest damn fools in the world. They are too easygoing and niggardly to prepare. Then at the last minute they hurry around and scrape together and fight like hell. Good luck has pulled them through. If the good Lord once forgets them, they will be finished."

Reminding himself of one of the many troubles he had to face—the British did not have a single capital ship left in either the Pacific or the Indian Ocean—one evening in the middle of a film he leaned over toward Harriman and, defending Admiral Phillips, who had gone down with his ship, remarked, "It is a sad business, the *Prince of Wales* and the *Repulse*. They could have harassed the enemy, always playing the second role to your big fleet. We made great sacrifices to send them [to Singapore]. They came in time. It is a cruel thing. But I will never criticize a man who aims his arrow at the enemy. I will defend him." And in his memoirs he would also defend himself of charges of "civilian interference" in sending them uselessly.

The noise and vibration in Churchill's personal quarters aft rendered it all but unusable, and he worked where he could. In a long letter to be mailed to his wife on arrival, he wrote to Clementine on Sunday, December 21, "I had been hoping till an hour ago to dine with the President tomorrow, Monday night—

and this is not yet impossible—but it is still blowing hard and from my porthole I can see, every minute, tremendous seas pouring over the bow of the ship, while down below can be heard the crash of them striking the sides. We are running obliquely across the waves and sometimes the ship rolls very heavily. However, once you get used to the motion, you don't care a damn."

Three days earlier he had told Clementine in a letter to be posted on shore as diplomatic mail, "We left our destroyer escort behind as they could not keep up with us in the rough seas." If the weather improved, they expected to pick up an American destroyer escort north of Bermuda that would guide the *Duke of York* into the Chesapeake Bay then north toward Annapolis.

There would be no American destroyers. None could cope with the heavy weather, which had so retarded the battleship itself that Lord Beaverbrook quipped that they might as well have traveled by submarine. Yet despite the risks and the turbulence, Churchill was relieved, he wrote, that he did not attempt to fly. He had been offered encouragement that a flight over the Atlantic to Nova Scotia would take only twelve or fourteen hours, but in winter "sometimes you are kept waiting 6, 8 or 10 days for favorable weather, so that the tortoise may still beat the hare." As Americans were not yet on ration coupons for clothing, he intended to cable Clementine on arrival "to know the length of your stockings." He was, after all, arriving at "Christmastide."

THAT THE PM WOULD actually be staying at the White House was unanticipated in the first hectic days after Pearl Harbor. Lord Halifax had been to the White House to press for accepting Churchill in Washington even before Adolf Hitler had announced that the Third Reich was at war with the United States.

Addressing the toothless Reichstag, convened only to listen to him, Hitler screamed at "that man who, while our soldiers are fighting in snow and ice . . . likes to make his chats from the fireside, the man who is the main culprit in this war." Churchill had been replaced in Berlin by a new target.

A visit by Churchill so soon after Pearl Harbor, Halifax had cabled Downing Street, might be "rather too strong medicine" for some American public opinion, which the President "still feels he has to educate up to the complete conviction of the oneness of the struggle against both Germany and Japan. . . . They are terribly shaken here, as you can well suppose, and fully realise that they have been caught napping."

The welcome offer to Churchill included dinner on the evening he reached dry land. It would be a somewhat different White House than George VI and Queen Elizabeth had visited in the sunny summer of 1939, just before the European war had broken out. Preparatory blackout curtains hung at each window; exterior lighting was dimmed and directed away from the walls. Sentry boxes were set up at driveway entrances and along the perimeter fences. Police patrolled where onlookers once strolled. Yet a stately Christmas tree was being erected on the White House lawn.

SECRETARY OF WAR HENRY STIMSON was instructed to prepare an American agenda for the visit, to be ready by the weekend before the British party arrived. He called together Chief of Staff George C. Marshall; Army Air Forces chief, Lieutenant General Henry H. ("Hap") Arnold; Chief of War Plans Leonard T. Gerow, a brigadier general; and his new deputy, Dwight D. Eisenhower, another one-star general assigned largely to Pacific operations, as he had served in the prewar Philippines and earlier in Washington under Douglas MacArthur. By December 20, a Saturday, a "Suggested Analysis of the Basic Topics and their Attendant Problems" was submitted to the White House. It largely reaffirmed Churchill's views that Germany was the prime enemy and that "a violent renewal of submarine activity" in the North Atlantic had to be anticipated. Stimson, however, realized that with Pearl Harbor the precipitant of American involvement, the public would want evidence of some action against the Japanese, who were sweeping through Southeast Asia and were already in the Philippines.

A joint Anglo-American board in Washington since March 1941, with little but an advisory function, met on Sunday the 21st to evaluate what might be done with so little time and re-sources already diminished by attacks, invasions, materiel losses, and defeats across the globe. It could only recommend "hold[ing] where necessary while building up strength." Yet even holding was nearly impossible. That Sunday afternoon at a conference at the White House, with the Secretaries of War and Navy (Henry Stimson and Frank Knox) and their top brass, the President went over the memoranda item by item, reviewing how their recom-mendations fit the burgeoning bad news. The "big fleet" Chur-chill had referred to was no longer big. Dockside Pearl Harbor was a ruin, although repair facilities and fuel storage tanks had not been impacted, and two aircraft carriers normally moored there had been at sea and were happily unscathed. Despite nine hours' warning after Pearl Harbor, General MacArthur had more than half his air force destroyed on the ground. Tons of his un-protected supplies had burned on the docks at Cavite, near Manila. He had made little or no provision to protect food, fuel, and munitions stocks for withdrawals, and the ongoing invasion of Luzon at Lingayen Gulf, first reported falsely as thwarted, was a reality. The pitiful Asian fleet based in Manila Bay was scattered or sunk. Guam was gone. The American presence in the Pacific barely existed.

Isolated Hong Kong had been penetrated from its Kowloon Peninsula and New Territories appendages on the mainland. Its fall was expected by Christmas. The outcome was never in doubt. At Sandy Ridge in Lo Wu in the New Territories, Lieutenant Colonel Robert A. MacPherson lay among twenty casualties. Sadism was far from uncommon among Japanese soldiery, especially when they tasted victory. The wounded were savagely beaten with rifle butts, roped together in threes, and bayoneted. Sergeant Major Matthew C. Hamlon, with three riflemen of the Royal Rifles of Canada were captured at Eucliff. Stripped of their weapons, their hands were bound behind their backs. Prodded forward with bayonets to the edge of a cliff, they were made to sit down, seeing below the bodies of previous dead, some beheaded. Colonel Roji Tanaka ordered a firing squad forward and all were shot, but Hamlon rolled down the cliff and survived to testify at the war crimes trial of the colonel years later.

Realizing only that the entire Hong Kong scene was an irreversible tragedy, Churchill wrote, "Although one knew it was a forlorn outpost, we expected that they would hold out on the fortified island for a good many weeks, possibly for several months." But "fortified" exaggerated the reality. For a token defense, a British historian has written, absorbing as many casualties as would happen before surrender was absurd. "At the very most all that would be required was a[n infantry] company, bugler, flag corporal, and a suave governor with a knighthood, double-barrelled name, stiff upper lip–and a tie from one of the lesser public schools."

After landing in Malaya nearly unopposed, the Japanese were moving southward toward the Johore Strait and Singapore. The British had nearly no navy left in Singapore, and what remained of its pathetic air force was so obsolete that Lieutenant General

Arthur E. Percival's forlorn attempt to hold the northern Kra air-fields was senseless. The Japanese had, Churchill conceded, "an unlimited power of reinforcement." Their timetable specified crossing the broad Perak River on the 15th; the occupation of Kuala Lumpur, the major city in Malaya, a month later; arrival at Johore Baru across the strait from Singapore on January 31; and the taking of Singapore itself on February 11, the date chosen because it was the anniversary of the coronation of the mythical Emperor Jimmu in 660 BC. The schedule was only slightly more ambitious than the reality. By December 21 they had reached the Perak River. To the east, Burma had been penetrated, and Thailand quickly occupied with hardly a shot fired.

Escorted by the cruiser *Pensacola*, the American convoy of slow transports that had been lumbering southwest from Honolulu to reinforce the Philippines could no longer get there and had been rerouted toward Australia. (It reached Brisbane on the 22nd.) The western Pacific had become a Japanese pond. The five thousand troops, seventy planes, forty-eight 75-mm guns, 340 trucks, six hundred tons of bombs, nine thousand barrels of aviation fuel, and 3,500,000 rounds of ammunition had nowhere else to go. Troops on Luzon still thought that all of it was coming their way. The MacArthur propaganda line from rapidly emptying Manila, voicing false optimism, empty hope, and certain victory, was being echoed in the American press and had to be cautiously addressed to deflect dismay. As a result, MacArthur, having done almost nothing, was becoming a hero for fighting a rear-guard action in terrain he had never visited. Yet to Churchill, "The entry of the United States into the war is worth all the losses sustained in the East many times over." The British were coming to Washington, which had made the war sustainable, to plan the long road back.

December 22, 1941

For the Japanese, "X-Day" had been the simultaneous attacks across the Pacific and Southeast Asia on December 8, Tokyo time—December 7 across the International Date Line at Pearl Harbor. In his diary Admiral Matome Ugaki, bullet-domed chief of staff to Isoroku Yamamoto, planner of "Strike South," referred to December 22 as "X + 14." Responding that day to the congratulatory message of Yoshiki Takamura, Yamamoto explained, "That we could defeat the enemy at the outbreak of the war was because they were unguarded and also they made light of us. 'Danger comes sooner when it is despised' and 'Don't despise a small enemy' are really important. I think they can be applied not only to wars but to routine matters."

Both admirals' flags flew from the battleship *Nagato* in Kure harbor, below Hiroshima on the southern end of the big island of Honshu. "At 0500," Ugaki wrote—it was still the 21st in the United States—"our Philippine Assault Forces entered Lingayen Bay and landed there safe and sound. . . . They encountered no enemy resistance. I sense that the enemy has lost her fighting spirit." Smaller landings in the north of Luzon had been unopposed. Japanese newspapers quoting sources in the West, Ugaki reported, "say the United States will defend Singapore even after they abandon the Philippines. But can those who once have abandoned the Philippines keep Singapore? I very much doubt it.

And Hong Kong has not many days left. I don't doubt that Singapore will fall sooner than we expect."

At 2:35 A.M. Wake Island time, according to American accounts, the Japanese were engaging marines on the beaches in clashes that, Admiral Shigetaro Shimada, the naval minister wrote, "would have made the gods weep." American Task Force 14 under Admiral Frank Jack Fletcher, steaming to the rescue from Hawaii, was more than four hundred miles away and was ordered, uselessly, by Admiral William Pye, who was in temporary command at Pearl Harbor, to remain at least two hundred miles distant to protect the carrier *Saratoga* from enemy bombers. A red flare from the shoreline signaled to Japanese transports that the first wave had landed. The marines at Wilkes Island (claw-shaped Wake was the central island of three small reefs) had only 2 three-inch guns as well as their Thompson submachine guns to fire at the landing barges in the predawn darkness. In the glare of their two searchlights the invaders kept coming.

Many of Lieutenant General Masaharu Homma's landing craft at Lingayen on Luzon included bicycles (as in Malaya) as well as troops, as he was confident from fifth-columnist reports that soldiers could pedal down toward Manila without much resistance. To ensure that, although the skies were dark and an intermittent rain falling, fighter planes machine-gunned the handful of defenders in beach barrios. Then light tanks and motorized artillery lumbered ashore from succeeding landing craft. Troops that had landed earlier at Aparri to the north moved down to meet them, running into resistance only from Filipino training squads fifty miles inland, then firing and bayoneting through. In a few instances overconfident Japanese units marched southward in parade formation, with Rising Sun flags flying and bands playing, and scattering when a few American P-40s attacked. Reorganizing, the Japanese plodded on until nightfall.

IN FRIGID MOSCOW Anthony Eden's private secretary, Oliver Harvey, noted in his diary, "We left the station [for Murmansk] at 6"—evening in Russia, morning in America—"after A.E. had a final goodbye meeting with Stalin. [Foreign Minister V. M.] Molotov saw us off and we got back into the same train which had brought us. Bands and guards of honour as before. Our meals on the train got rather mixed up. We had what we thought was a cold Sunday supper about 7—and then it turned out only to be tea and we were threatened with a large dinner at 8.30. This we refused, and went early to bed."

Long warned not to send Christmas cards, as Nazism was in effect the new religion of the *Reich*, Germans were now forbidden to waste valuable paper by sending New Year's cards, which had become a covert substitute. As minister of information and czar of public communication, Joseph Goebbels had already forbidden radio stations to play traditional Christmas hymns, with "*O Tannenbaum*" excepted, as its words made no reference to the holiday. Small tabletop Christmas trees had been a tradition for more than two hundred years, but trees were scarce, and their decoration—even with rationed candles—would create suspicion.

IN WASHINGTON on Monday morning, December 22, the President, armed with newspapers, mail, and messages, planned to breakfast, as usual, in bed. Eleanor—as she was not on her own elsewhere—arrived at his bedside to tick off her own itinerary.

FDR's confidential messages were far more dreary than the trio of headlines in the *New York Times*, which published what was released to reporters and wire sources, or had passed army and navy censorship:

80 JAPANESE TRANSPORTS APPEAR OFF LUZON

U.S. SANK OR DAMAGED 14 U-BOATS IN ATLANTIC

HITLER OUSTS ARMY HEAD, TAKES FULL CONTROL

The Japanese were landing 43,000 troops at Lingayen Gulf, and MacArthur's communiqués were nothing but boastful fiction or damage control to prepare the public for the worst. Army personnel on Luzon numbered about 15,000, plus 65,000 poorly trained and inadequately armed Filipinos, the best of them the Philippine Scouts. The German subs sunk off the Atlantic coast were equally fictitious, nothing more than depth charges dropped near suspected quarry that might have been fish. Hitler had indeed taken control of the *Wehrmacht* to forbid further withdrawals on the frigid Russian front. The newspapers set before the President would not report the end of resistance on Wake Island for two more days, but Admiral Ugaki's diary on the 23rd—nearly a day earlier in Washington—recorded epic resistance by the overwhelmed marine garrison:

> One of the hardest nuts to crack, the attack on Wake Island, might have been finished this morning, but contrary to my expectations, no report has come out. Not only the senior staff but all of the staff were almost impatient. At last, about 1100, a telegram message came that the attacks had been made. They approached the coast at 0035, began to land against furious en-

emy resistance, besides high seas. At about 1100 the occupation . . . was finished. This is a great relief.

It had been an unexpectedly difficult episode and did not con-
clude as rapidly as reported. The Japanese had lost twelve times
as many dead as had the Wake defenders, a submarine sunk with
all hands, and also the destroyer *Hayate.* Ugaki added his sympathy for the commander of the Fourth Fleet "for the awkward position into which he was thrown." He feared the admiral's suicide.

The new giant battleship *Yamato,* at 73,590 tons displace-
ment, the largest capital ship afloat, with long-range 18.1-inch
guns, had just completed its shakedown trials and had entered
Kure harbor, anchoring west of the *Nagato.* Ugaki went aboard to
inspect it. He was not satisfied. It had been designed with "old
ideas."* Airborne torpedoes had sunk the *Prince of Wales* and the
Repulse in "the Malay Sea Battle," but the admiral mused hope-
fully that "big guns will have their chance some day."

The President's chief butler, Alonzo Fields, reaching Roosevelt's bedroom, was surprised to hear, floating out the door, Mrs.
Roosevelt's normally correct if not affectionate voice objecting,
"Why didn't you tell me? I can't find Mrs. Nesbitt anywhere. If
only I had known . . ." Henrietta Nesbitt was the White House
head cook—*chef* was a term too elevated for her menus.

Roosevelt noticed Fields waiting warily at the door and lowered the emotional temperature slightly. "Now, Eleanor, all that
little woman would do even if she were here is to tell Fields what
we can tell him ourselves right now. Fields, at eight tonight we

---

*One of the "old ideas" may have been inadequate anti-aircraft protection.
Yamato participated (distantly) in the Battle of Midway in June 1942 and was
used sparingly thereafter. It was sunk by American torpedo planes in May
1945 as it was suicidally heading toward Okinawa.

have to have dinner ready for twenty. Mr. Churchill and his party are coming to stay with us for a few days."

Both Roosevelts expected the Prime Minister and his party, but because of their delays at sea and the understanding that he would cruise up the Potomac from his anchorage, Churchill was scheduled to arrive the next day. Yet his impulsive request for a plane had altered matters. For security reasons, the President had not wanted to alert the White House staff too soon, and Mrs. Roosevelt fussed that she had not yet allocated rooms nor arranged for a dinner with the additional high-level guests her husband wanted. The PM's arrival was also cutting into her scheduled press conference at 9:30. She was extraordinarily busy, writing a syndicated newspaper column ("My Day"), giving speeches as First Lady, making inspection tours, representing a wheelchair-bound president, and working as unpaid assistant director (under the feisty and controversial Fiorello LaGuardia) of the Office of Civil Defense.

The inauspicious beginning of the day may have made the President unusually sharp with his first official visitor. At 10:50 he expected the new Soviet ambassador, Maxim Litvinov, who was accompanied by former US envoy to Russia, William Bullitt. The stocky, sixtyish Litvinov, Lenin's first ambassador to Britain after the revolution and dismissed by Stalin as foreign minister because of his Jewish origins during the cynical rapprochement with Hitler, had been rehabilitated. (The veteran Bolshevik V. M. Molotov proved more acceptable to Berlin.) When Averell Harriman, with Lord Beaverbrook, had been on a supply mission to Moscow, Harriman had been "shocked" by Litvinov's appearance. (He had been summoned hastily to interpret for Stalin.) "His clothes and shoes were shoddy and, I remember, his waistcoat and trousers did not meet to cover the expanse of his shirt front." On arrival in New York, Litvinov, now back in precarious favor, had purchased more suitable clothing for his new role. When he presented himself to Roosevelt in three-piece Madison Avenue garb, FDR, extending his hand, asked, "You get that suit in Moscow?"

Realizing the envoy's background and hoping that he would be more than a toady for the Kremlin, Roosevelt reached out for some idealism, hoping that Litvinov would want to be remembered for something positive. To Litvinov's discomfort, the President remarked, rather rudely, "Some day you will die and you will probably know beforehand that you are to die and you will remember your parents and all that they meant to you, and what then?" Litvinov confessed to Bullitt as they left that it was a poor beginning. He didn't like the President's hectoring yet had to put up with it. His job was to extract as much Lend-Lease war materiel for Russia as was possible and to minimize long-simmering anti-Soviet feeling in America. Thanks to Hitler and Hirohito, Litvinov's country had become an ally.

Roosevelt had other ceremonial duties after Litvinov withdrew. The President received the Chinese ambassador, Hu Shih, a noted philosopher but largely a figurehead for the family of Chiang Kaishek and his wife; and Netherlands envoy Alexander Loudon. Then, after lunch with Harry Hopkins, who, however frail and chronically ailing, had long been FDR's primary link to Britain and managed Lend-Lease; then Roosevelt telephoned the Canadian Prime Minister, William Lyon Mackenzie King, to confirm that "a certain person" was "on his way." Aware it was happening, King had invited Churchill to make a quick trip to Ottawa to address the Canadian parliament and planned to come to Washington to escort him. "There will have to be a Supreme Council," Roosevelt told King, "and I am determined that it shall have its headquarters in Washington."

With a large French-speaking population in Quebec and realizing its sensitivities, King would soon have fraying relations with the Vichy rump of defeated France to plague him. For Roosevelt, the issue was German influence on the unoccupied quarter of

29

France. With its vast colonial empire almost intact, collaborationist Vichy was under pressure to submit to whatever the Nazi regime wanted, under threat of cutting off food supplies or even of a full takeover. America's major French prize, the big liner *Normandie*, docked in Manhattan after 139 Atlantic crossings since 1935, had been requisitioned by the United States after the surrender of France in 1940. It was almost like seizing a piece of French territory.

Worried about German occupation, the State Department ordered American ambassador Admiral William D. Leahy, an old FDR friend from the Great War years and since, to send eight staffers and all confidential files in Vichy to the embassy in Switzerland. Press and radio censorship, Leahy cabled Roosevelt on the 22nd, left "Japanese treachery" at Pearl Harbor "completely unknown here" and had no influence on popular French feeling. The seizure of the *Normandie* and its being refitted as a troopship, now rechristened the *Lafayette*,* "had produced no violent reaction whatever," Leahy reported from talks with the Vichy resident generals in Tunisia and Morocco. The liner's reuse had long been expected.

Leahy reported, more than Vichy knew, "that Germany is suffering a major defeat in Russia and is rapidly approaching a similar but more complete military reverse in [colonial] Cyrenaica"—Libya. The Germans would have to rescue the situation there for the inept Italians, which might also mean *Wehrmacht* intervention in French North Africa. The subject was certain to turn up in Anglo-American discussions.

---

*The once-magnificent liner, set afire by a welder's torch on February 9, 1942, would be destroyed beyond saving. After the war it was sold for scrap.

HALF A DAY AHEAD IN TIME, the British in Malaya had blown all the bridges across the broad, muddy Perak, abandoning several thousand dismayed Indian troops on the north bank. "The British Army," Colonel Masanobu Tsuji wrote wryly, "excels in retreat." The Japanese began constructing pontoon bridges and brought up collapsible motor launches. While his new ally was prospering in semitropical Southeast Asia, to Hitler's frustration and outrage, reverses were afflicting the Germans deep into frigid Russia. Backtracking in snow and ice from untenable forward positions was not permitted by his edict but was nevertheless a fact of survival. His chief of staff, General Franz Halder, noted in his diary, "an exceedingly difficult situation has developed here, and it is beyond anyone's power to say how it will be restored. And yet it is impossible to prevail upon the Führer to order any long-range withdrawal."

PRESIDENTIAL PRESS SECRETARY Steve Early announced Churchill's arrival at 6:45 P.M. It was past seven in Washington when cameramen camped in the White House were able to pop flashbulbs and photograph Churchill and Roosevelt on the south portico. The President had a cane in his right hand, with his left arm gripping the arm of his naval aide, Captain John R. Beardall. Churchill wore a navy cap and heavy double-breasted sea overcoat. Before reporters could rush to telephones, Early handed them a brief statement for the morning papers: "The British Prime Minister has arrived in the United States to discuss with the President all questions related to the concerted war effort. Mr. Churchill is accompanied by Lord Beaverbrook and a technical staff. Mr. Churchill is a guest of the President." Newspapermen could add background color and speculation.

Franklin D. Roosevelt greets Prime Minister Winston Churchill on his arrival to the United States, December 22, 1941.
Franklin D. Roosevelt Presidential Library

Although his sea attire was a clue, how the PM got to Washington was unstated.

The news emerged quickly. By 10:30 P.M. one-cent Jefferson-
head postcards imprinted by the Fidelity Stamp Company in
Washington with

WINSTON CHURCHILL

British Prime Minister

ARRIVES

at the

WHITE HOUSE

December 22, 1941

were being sold and postmarked at the Benjamin Franklin postal
station.

Before the "important visitor" had appeared, Steve Early reminded reporters of the Censorship Act. A later White House update added, "There is, of course, one primary objective in the conversations to be held in the next few days between the President and the British Prime Minister and the respective staffs of the two countries. That purpose is the defeat of Hitlerism throughout the world." The statement noted that other allied nations would be consulted, and further announcements would be forthcoming, but the focus of Churchill's planning scenarios radioed ahead had already been implicitly accepted. Despite the overwhelming American antipathy toward what seemed an unstoppable Japan, the term *Hitlerism* made it clear that victory over Germany had to come first.

Even before Churchill sat down to a late dinner at the White House, a report in *The Times* of London had appeared, obviously emanating from Downing Street, that the PM's mission had been "his own idea" and that, as coordination among partners was crucial, he was "not the only British statesman who is at present out of the country." It was a strong hint rising through the secrecy that Foreign Secretary Anthony Eden was already long absent from London and very likely on a circuitous journey to meet with Stalin in Moscow. Eden had left for Scotland the day after Pearl Harbor to join a task force sailing to Murmansk over the hazardous subarctic supply route arcing over Norway and Finland. The icy waters were infested with U-boats. Eden had cautioned Churchill, who had proposed going to Washington, "that I could not see how we could both be away at once. He said we could. The emphasis of the war had shifted; what now mattered was the intentions of our two great allies. We must each go to one of them."

The PM was still aboard the *Duke of York* approaching the East Coast when, on December 21, he received a radio encrypt from Eden in Moscow that, as the price of cooperation, Stalin, optimistic now that Germany could be turned back, had demanded secret Allied acceptance of prewar Soviet encroachments in Europe. The Red Army had seized the Baltic states in 1940, taken territory from Finland, and former Czarist territory from Romania, Czechoslovakia, and Poland. Although all of it was now occupied by the *Wehrmacht,* the Soviets expected to outlast Hitler. "Stalin, I believe," Eden added, "sincerely wants military agreements, but he will not sign until we recognize his frontiers, and we must expect badgering on this issue." Churchill radioed his Deputy Prime Minister, Clement Attlee, that the demands violated the Atlantic Charter, "to which Stalin has subscribed," and in any case no arrangement could be made "without prior agreement with the United States."

Stalin's contempt for pieces of diplomatic paper and confidence about the Red Army's future control of the ground in question would keep the absorbed territories in the grip of Stalin's successors until the implosion of the Soviet Union decades later. Churchill advised Attlee not to be "downhearted" if Eden should leave Moscow "without any flourish of trumpets." And to Eden he conceded in a radiogram, "Naturally you will not be rough with Stalin," but there could be no "secret and special pacts" without the United States. Even to present Stalin's demands to Roosevelt (who, as would his successors, never recognize the theft of Estonia, Latvia, and Lithuania) would be "to court a blank refusal" and "lasting trouble on both sides."

Churchill had already radioed Stalin "sincere wishes for your birthday"—he would be sixty-two on December 21. In return, Stalin offered the PM and the British army "my sincere congratulations in connection with your recent victories in Libya." At a birthday banquet in the Kremlin Eden reported as Churchill was reaching United States waters, "We drank [to] your health and some others. Stalin spoke very warmly of you." On returning, Eden would tell Brooke that state dinners in Moscow began at ten and lasted until five. "[General] Timoshenko arrived drunk and by continuous drinking restored himself to sobriety by 5 A.M. On the other hand, [Marshal] Voroshilov after at least arriving sober, had to be carried out before the evening was over." Before the Marshal slumped down, Stalin—who prudently watered his vodka—asked Eden, "Do your Generals also hold their drink so badly?"

Diplomatically, Eden answered, like Stalin through an interpreter standing by, "They may have a better capacity for drink, but they have not the same ability for winning battles!"

Much was on Churchill's figurative plate as he prepared for a late dinner at the White House. Despite her outburst at breakfast, Eleanor Roosevelt had greeted him and her husband warmly as they emerged from the elevator on the second floor. Weary from attending pre-Christmas activities all over Washington through the day, she had returned to oversee room arrangements for Churchill and his small airborne party. She showed Lord Beaverbrook to a bedroom, the PM's deputy Tommy Thompson to another, the Yellow Bedroom, and John Martin, the PM's private secretary, to the Small Blue Bedroom. The two Scotland Yard shadows were given a joint room and Churchill's valet a dressing room adjoining Churchill's quarters. The Monroe Room, Eleanor explained to Churchill, had been emptied of furniture to serve as his map room, to parallel his planning domain in the Cabinet War Rooms, underground below buildings at the corner of Great George Street and Storey's Gate. (He would shortly have the Monroe Room covered with maps and colored pins, showing the movements of British troops and ships.)

A tale more likely apocryphal is that she showed him to the fabled Lincoln Bedroom, which he proceeded, without informing her, to dislike. Once she left, he allegedly tried out beds in other rooms and selected for himself the Rose Bedroom, next to Thompson's room on the east end of the floor. It was decorated with Victorian scenes and, whether or not he knew its history, had been used by Queen Elizabeth on her visit in 1939. According to Harry Hopkins's close friend and FDR speechwriter Robert Sherwood, however, Churchill was "installed in the big [Rose] bedroom across from Hopkins' room, and as the two of them walked back and forth to visit one another they had to pick their way through great piles of Christmas parcels." Hopkins, a widower and FDR's trusted intimate—almost his second self—lived in the White House with his daughter, Diana, then nine. Son of a harness-maker in Sioux City, Iowa, he had been described to Churchill warily, in traditional Tory fashion, before he met and bonded decisively with Hopkins, as "the old nonconformist conscience of Victorian liberalism. . . . He does not believe that a world in which some live in the sun and others in the shadows makes sense."

Mrs. Roosevelt had invited the advance party to "tea" at 8:15 in the ground floor Red Room while dinner was being prepared, but recognizing Churchill's lack of eagerness for the signature British beverage, FDR was already seated at a small table prepared to mix more potent drinks. The PM emerged in one of his characteristic guises—the blue cap and (over a ruffled shirt) the double-breasted coat of an Elder Brother of Trinity House, the venerable guild chartered by Henry VIII and headquartered at Tower Hill, still supporting lighthouses and navigational aids. To be one of the thirty-one elite Elder Brothers was a valued royal, naval, or political distinction.

The President prized his special martini recipe, although its mild relative proportions were often considered by guests to be unfortunate, and he also offered other mixed libations, including one with dark Haitian rum. Gin concoctions were long associated with Britain and, indeed, the empire, but Churchill's tastes ran to sherry, whiskey, brandy, and champagne, beginning on awakening, and none adulterated by flavored, nonalcoholic ingredients. As additional guests arrived, the President had a trolley rolled in with caviar, smoked turkey, smoked clams, and assorted cheeses, all now rarities in London.

Dinner was served in the long dining room. Ambassador Lord Halifax had arrived, joining Secretary of State Cordell Hull and Mrs. Hull, Under Secretary of State Sumner Welles and Mrs. Welles, Harry Hopkins, Lord Beaverbrook and several close Roosevelt friends, such as Mrs. "Bertie" Hamlin. Henrietta Nesbitt, whose bland cuisine often caused presidential invitees to pass up a White House dinner, furnished broiled chicken and vegetables, with a dessert of strawberry shortcake and vanilla ice cream. (As the war wore on, because chicken did not require soon-to-be issued meat-ration coupons, she would serve fowl in some form almost daily.) Closing the light banter over dinner, the President raised a goblet of champagne. "I have a toast to offer," he began, "—it has been in my head and on my heart now for a long time—now it is on the tip of my tongue—'To the common cause.'"

It was already ten o'clock. As the waiters and maids began collecting plates and glasses, the President wheeled his chair about and was propelled toward the green-carpeted Oval Office, with Churchill, Beaverbrook, Halifax, Hopkins, Welles, and Hull following and taking seats on the brown and green leather chairs once salvaged from Theodore Roosevelt's yacht *Mayflower*. A general discussion began, as prologue to meetings scheduled for the morning of December 23. Churchill knew the answer before he asked his initial question: Would the President concede to public desire to go directly after Japan? The PM knew that distances, and resources, made that impractical. The priority, he was assured, was "Europe first." Both agreed that Americans had to get into some action that was not wholly defensive as soon as possible, and that meant across the Atlantic—probably French North Africa, whether or not the puppet Pétain regime in Vichy resisted. Georges Mandel, Minister of the Interior until the armistice with Germany, described the aged Marshal Henri Philippe Pétain ironically as "*le conquistador,*" playing on "*le con qui se dort*"—the fool who is asleep.

As the Oval Office emptied at about midnight, Churchill recalled, "I wheeled [the President] in his chair from the drawing room to the lift as a mark of respect and thinking also of Sir Walter Raleigh spreading his cloak before Queen Elizabeth."

EARLY EDITIONS OF the morning newspapers had been delivered, and those in the White House knew much more than the press was permitted to print. One problem that would plague American war industry could not be concealed and had already made the front pages. Welders and other laborers in San Francisco Bay–area shipyards were striking. The army had to be called in to "prevent molestation" of those willing to work. The Japanese already in Luzon were moving, more rapidly than reported, south from Lingayen Gulf and north from Lamon Bay, closing in on undefended Manila. Handouts from MacArthur about the capital contended otherwise.

Outnumbered but feisty marines on Wake Island were close to surrender. Commander Winfield Scott Cunningham radioed Admiral Pye and Admiral Fletcher tersely: "ENEMY ON ISLAND. ISSUE IN DOUBT." Pearl Harbor ordered Task Force 14 to reverse course and return. Marine pilots on the flight deck of the *Saratoga* banged their fists against their planes and wept openly. Major James Devereux on Wake sent orders where he could: "Cease firing and destroy all weapons. The island is being surrendered." On its Wilkes outcrop, unaware of the grim situation on

Wake itself, sixty marines fought on uselessly with their bolt-action 1903 Springfields. A chunk of shrapnel scraped the scalp of Private First Class Artie Stocks after ripping off his British-style World War I–vintage helmet and lodged in the bank behind him. He picked it up. Embossed on the fragment was the identification, "Made in Ohio USA." American companies until ordered to cease had profited from scrap metal sales to Japan.

Frustration abounded. U-boats had begun torpedoing tankers so close to the brightly lit Atlantic and Gulf of Mexico seaboards—fine target background not yet blacked out—that watchers ashore could see ships ablaze. (And five more submarines would leave pens on the Bay of Biscay on Christmas Day.) Hong Kong's beleaguered and backtracking garrison was still gamely "holding out."

According to published reports from General MacArthur, American and Filipino troops had the situation in Luzon "well in hand," which was, as Washington knew, unrealistic at best, as was his claim that many Japanese troop transports had been sunk by coast artillery and tanks. No artillery had defended the landing sites, and no tanks. Only carefully vetted reports from correspondents were permitted through MacArthur's censorship. For the North American Newspaper Alliance, Royal Arch Gunnison reported under a Nichols Field dateline—the airbase had been devastated by Japanese bombers—that he was permitted to state that Nichols Field had been "lightly bombed" and that the morale of ground crews was "excellent." He saw "three mud-covered green-dungaree boys" lifting a wounded comrade out of a machine-gun pit. It was "nothing much," the injured soldier told Gunnison, "just a slight burn here in the side." One of the others in the ground crew "cursed the Japanese in the most complete manner I have ever heard anyone told off"—perhaps a clue to what really occurred at Nichols Field, soon to be abandoned.

MacArthur's own regal communiqués, largely self-aggrandizing fantasy, made him a headlines hero. Of 142 issued by his head-quarters before his escape to Australia on March 11, 1942, 109 communiqués identified only one person—Douglas MacArthur.

———— ∞∞∞ ————

FROM HIS BEDROOM Churchill dictated to John Martin a telegram to the British War Cabinet in London. "There was general agreement," he noted,

> that if Hitler was held in Russia he must try something else, and that the most probable line was Spain and Portugal en route to North Africa. . . . There was general agreement that it was vital to forestall the Germans. . . . The President said that he was anxious that American land forces should give their support as quickly as possible wherever they could be most helpful, and favoured the idea of a plan to move into North Africa being pre-pared . . . with or without [Vichy French] invitation.
>
> It was agreed to remit the study of the project to Staffs. . . . It was recognised that shipping was plainly a most important fac-tor. . . . In the course of conversation the President mentioned that he would propose at forthcoming conference that United States should relieve our troops in Northern Ireland, and spoke of sending three or four divisions there. I warmly welcomed this, and said I hope that one of the divisions would be an armoured division. It was not thought that this need conflict with prepara-tions for a United States force for North Africa.

Lord Halifax returned to his embassy worried about "how re-mote my mind and thoughts are from Winston's and Max [Beaverbrook]'s." Realizing how unprepared the United States remained, Churchill's positive slant on future operations as he intended to guide them appalled Halifax. He worried whether the PM by force of personality and experience of war, however flawed, could impose his strategic ideas on the Americans. Churchill had failed in Norway in 1940 and again in Greece, to even heavier losses, earlier in 1941. Events had thrust Halifax from prewar Appeasement, but he harbored doubts about what might be done, where, and how fast. It was quite enough, the PM thought, that the Americans, with their potential, were now in the fight. "I was terribly shocked by Winston's growth in the egotistic habit of thought. 'I can do this: I won't do that, etc., etc.'" Halifax retired to sleep, as did the denizens of the White House. Churchill could not.

December 23, 1941

ABOARD THE DESTROYER *Akigumo* in the Pearl Harbor strike force returning to Japan, Lieutenant Commander Sadao Chigusa, the executive officer (later a rear admiral), wrote in his diary just after dawn on the 24th (a day earlier across the Date Line), "At last we are in the very day of our arrival at our motherland. It was very fine weather after a typhoon had passed." The fleet was poised to enter Bungo Suido Channel between the southern islands of Shikoku and Kyushu en route to Kure on Honshu, and by 7:30 he could see, dimly, the mountains of Shikoku. He felt "deeply moved." By 9:30 patrol aircraft from the mainland were "dancing in the air over our fleet." General Quarters was called so that crew not immediately needed could crowd the decks to savor the homecoming. It was a happy gathering. They had already learned that the Hawaiian voyage had earned each seaman a bonus of two months' pay over his regular salary.

Sailors had their lunch at noon and an hour later entered the Inland Sea, casting anchor at the Hashirajima berth in Hiroshima Bay. Chigusa's ship was the last destroyer to dock. "With great relief I could feel refreshed in body and mind and took my first bath in over one month. . . . All officers gathered in the wardroom and drank a toast to our success in the Battle and congratulated each other. . . ."

RELATIONS WERE MUCH LESS WARM with their new allies, the Germans. Neither side trusted the other, although a thriving business existed in trading in raw materials like rubber, which the *Reich* needed for war equipment the Japanese could import or copy. The Germans also wanted the newest Japanese torpedoes that had been so successful at Pearl Harbor, and the "more than 20 British aerial torpedoes" captured by the Japanese in Malaya at Kota Bharu. Admiral Paul Wenneker, the German naval attaché in Tokyo, was asked in exchange "about the state of completion of the German aircraft carrier *Graf Zeppelin*. The Japanese Navy would welcome it if this vessel could be transferred. They do not think," Wenneker wrote, "that the vessel can play any role in the conduct of German naval strategy any longer. . . . If the vessel could be brought to the Pacific under Japanese control, it can play a much greater role. I advised [Vice Admiral Minoru] Maeda to arrange for the subject to be discussed in Berlin."

Flugzeugträger A—the unfinished *Graf Zeppelin*—was the farthest along of two carriers that the German admiralty had been building at Baltic ports. Hitler had ordered work stopped in order to conserve manpower and steel for U-boats, then restarted, then halted again, but he refused to let the warship out of German hands. The British had bombed it once, unsuccessfully. It would be scuttled in harbor in 1945, then raised by the Russians. Its hulk was towed to Leningrad to be scrapped.

German freighters long at sea ran the porous British blockade, usually flying spurious foreign flags, from Bordeaux and around Cape Horn into the South Pacific east of New Zealand and up through the Japanese-mandated Carolines and Marianas to Yokohama. (Italian freighters also slipped through, including one then in port, the *Orseolo*.) Despite the risks taken by the *Kriegs-*

marine, Admiral Wenneker had constant bureaucratic tangles with Japanese ministries regarding customs, finances, and security. The newest problem was that of the freighter *Rio Grande,* "to make it possible for the crew to be allowed to go ashore at last. . . . The German side cannot permit this kind of [suspicious] treatment toward the other ships expected to arrive here" and for permission "to make the return trip as soon as possible." Its cargo had yet to be unloaded. Wenneker worried about American submarines now reported offshore—although he would have worried less had he known how faulty their fuses were.

BY EVENING, his Fourteenth Army slowed in high seas, General Homma had landed all his forces aboard transports in Lingayen Bay, but he had not yet come ashore himself. Ordered out of hazardous Manila Bay toward the Dutch East Indies, Admiral Thomas Hart's pathetic Asian Fleet remnant of three cruisers and twelve destroyers, most of them four-stackers of World War I or postwar vintage, were voyaging toward Surabaja in eastern Java. Many would not survive the first months of engagement. Their first port of call had been Balikpapan on the southeastern coast of Borneo, where the destroyers *Ford* and *Pope* received a flash-lamp message from Lieutenant (jg) Henry F. Burfeind: "Greetings to my fellow [Annapolis] classmates. Left *Pillsbury* in Manila, ordered to *Mareschal Joffre* to take her south. See you in Surabaja." The unmilitary *Mareschal Joffre* was a 14,500-ton, rat-infested Vichy French freighter with a foreign crew who knew no English that was seized by American authorities when the war began. An ensign and twenty-eight enlisted sailors, most of whom had been wounded in the bombing of the Cavite naval base, were added to Burfeind's crew. En route to Balikpapan it was scouted by two Japanese planes, then left alone. It would continue on to Australia and New Zealand with its Chinese and Indochinese crew and make it to pier 23 in San Francisco via a refueling stop at Acapulco in Mexico, where it would leave without paying a docking fee. In California it was converted into a troopship renamed the *Rochambeau*. Many of its foreign crew joined the navy there, were paid, and issued uniforms.

SAILING FROM the Thames Estuary was the nine thousand–ton Norwegian-flag tanker *Regnbue (Rainbow)*, empty but for ballast, ordered to load fuel at Corpus Christi, Texas. Harry Larsen, the chief engineer, complained as they raised anchor about the horrors at sea at Christmas without "newts or frewts or yin." The ship's chandler in London could supply no nuts or fruit, but a lighter had brought out a case of gin and two cases of whiskey. *New Yorker* journalist A. J. Liebling, hitching a ride home, was assured that although "ordinarily" no liquor was served aboard ship "except to pilots and immigration officers, Christmas was always an exception." The *Regnbue* proceeded in a column of eight, one of five groups, with four corvettes as escort. No one expected the ships to remain together in the stormy Atlantic.

"Much colder as we go north," Oliver Harvey of Anthony Eden's party wrote from their train toward Murmansk, and their risky convoy home. "Meals still muddled—we had two breakfasts in succession at 9.30 and 1.30 but no lunch. However we hope to get dinner straight."

To their south, the winter war had already gone on so unexpectedly long for the Germans—Hitler had expected it to be over by the time the first snows fell in Russia—that he had issued a much-belated proclamation from "Führer Headquarters," soon picked up worldwide when it was broadcast on Berlin radio:

> German Volk!
>
> While the German homeland is not directly threatened by the enemy, with the exception of air raids, . . . if the German Volk wishes to give something to its soldiers at Christmas, then it should give the warmest clothing that it can do without during the war. In peacetime, all of this can easily be replaced. In spite of all the winter equipment prepared by the leadership in the *Wehrmacht* and its individual branches, every soldier deserves so much more!

Acknowledging the existence of Christmas to make the appeal more subtle, Hitler was preparing the public to give until it hurt. In a further directive he decreed the death penalty for anyone "who gets rich" profiteering from the expected flood of offerings to be managed by Joseph Goebbels, who had persuaded Hitler to inaugurate the clothing drive. It could not have been easy for the Führer to switch from his usual arrogance to covert admission that things were suddenly going wrong.

IN OCCUPIED PARIS a grey German military vehicle stopped at the entrance to Shakespeare and Company, Sylvia Beach's cluttered bookshop at 18, rue de l'Odéon. A *Wehrmacht* officer wanted to confirm that a book he wanted—perhaps as a Christmas present—was still for sale. Enemy registration for Americans instituted after Pearl Harbor had closed on the 17th, but Miss Beach, a dowdy fifty-four and in France since 1920, was still in

Sylvia Beech below her Shakespeare and Company bookshop sign in Paris, 1942. *Courtesy Princeton University Special Collections*

precarious business. Indoors he demanded, in fluent English, "I want that copy of *Finnegans Wake* you've got in the window."

"Well," she retorted, "that's the only copy left in Paris, and you can't have it. . . . You don't know Joyce." She recalled his anger rising as he insisted, "But we admire James Joyce very much in Germany." Although she refused to sell the book, the officer, surprisingly, strode out rather than confiscate it, "got into his great car, his great military car, surrounded with other fellows in helmets, and drove away." She determined to hide it.

CHURCHILL'S REMAINING RETINUE debarked at Newport News from the *Duke of York* and received its first taste of wartime America on a special train to Washington, which arrived just after midnight. What they saw en route resembled nothing left behind in austere, battered wartime Britain. Through placid Virginia, lights of homes, highways, shops, and even outdoor Christmas trees flashed by almost eerily to travelers accustomed to blackouts. The PM's military secretary, General Hastings Ismay, had remained in London as Churchill's resident uniformed deputy, but Ismay's associate, Colonel Ian Jacob, shepherding the traveling party, recorded happily "a first-rate sandwich dinner consisting of cold chicken, two hard-boiled eggs, salad, coffee and fruit." Real eggs, rather than the powdered substitute, were rare at home.

At the Mayflower, where they arrived from Union Station in a fleet of cars, the lobby windows and doors had been blackout darkened, to their surprise after the blaze of lights elsewhere, and emergency first-aid supplies were visibly in reach in case of air raids no one expected. The VIP visitors were shown by the hotel management how to access whiskey, beer, and a substance for cooling them known as ice, and each was given fifty dollars in cash, courtesy of the State Department, for minimal essentials.

On the roof above the hotel's ten floors, night and day, were lookouts for air attacks, and some buildings nearby had anti-aircraft guns of dubious usefulness atop, largely to suggest that there was a war on. The Germans had no long-distance bombers and at best might be able to fire short-range shells from surfaced subs hazardously venturing close to shore. The morning news-papers, already available at the front desk, were fat bundles adver-tising feasts of luxuries on the inside pages and litanies of bad news, all from far away, on the front pages.

Waiting for the group was American air forces chief, Lieu-tenant General Henry H. ("Hap") Arnold, who pulled aside Charles Portal and "Bomber" Harris for a brief talk. Arnold wanted to emphasize that the United States "could not afford to see the Philippines pass by the board." He hoped to "build up our air strength in the Philippines, Australia and the Dutch East In-dies as rapidly as possible" and that "we would cram into Aus-tralia such airplanes, combat crews and other air force personnel as possible to get there by air, by boat, or any other way" to assist General MacArthur. Yet despite MacArthur's imaginative com-muniqués and Arnold's impulsive unrealism, the Philippines were unsalvageable.

Promoting Churchill's line, Portal pressed for control "of the whole North African shore of the Mediterranean." And he "looked forward," Arnold wrote in his minutes, "to the time when U.S. bombers could be stationed in England to help out their bombing effort."

Sir Charles Wilson, the PM's physician, had barely turned on the lights in his hotel room when the phone rang. Restlessly pac-ing the Rose Room, Churchill could not sleep. He wanted Wil-son to supply him with a sleeping pill if it would do no harm. Ferried by a White House car, he arrived within minutes and found his patient merely too agitated to relax. There was so much to do. Churchill had already torn through early editions of the morning papers. "He must have a good night," the doctor wrote in his diary. Wilson offered two barbiturate sleeping pills for "bottling up his excitement" and returned to the Mayflower.

Given the late arrivals and Churchill's usual late mornings, conferences were scheduled for the "forenoon." Armed with newspapers, mail, and messages, Roosevelt himself usually break-fasted in bed. His butler, Alonzo Fields, knocked on the Prime Minister's door and was invited in to find a tangle of bedclothes and the floor littered with newspapers. The Prime Minister was barefoot and in long underwear. "Now Fields," Churchill began, "we had a lovely dinner last night but I have a few orders for you. We want to leave here as friends, right? So I need you to listen." The PM wanted no talking or whistling in the corridors. (Fields was puzzled as there never was any.) Further, "I must have a tum-bler of sherry in my room before breakfast, a couple of glasses of scotch and soda before lunch and French champagne and 90-year-old brandy before I go to sleep at night."

"Yes, sir," said Fields, who was unlikely to run out to fetch ninety-year-old brandy.

Breakfast, Churchill instructed, as he donned a zippered RAF jumpsuit, long called by the amused British his "siren suit," had to include something hot—"eggs, bacon or ham, and toast"—and also "two kinds of cold meats with English mustard and two kinds of fruit plus a tumbler of sherry." He also expected prompt delivery of the red government dispatch boxes, symbols of high office, which would arrive from the British embassy. Fields kept his thoughts to himself and bowed out.

The private "forenoon" meeting at the White House, before many of the principals could be gathered, followed late breakfasts for Roosevelt, Churchill, and Harry Hopkins—a night prowler, like the PM. Also present was H. Freeman Matthews, head of European Affairs at the State Department. He had been on his way to London when recalled to assist Secretary Hull, who ar-rived as the meeting wound up. The subject was "Gymnast," the ambitious operation to occupy French North Africa. Although Churchill and Roosevelt hoped to induce General Maxime

Weygand, the rump Vichy government's army chief, to join the attempt, Matthews warned that Weygand's loyalty to Pétain would cause any intervention to backfire. Weygand would refuse to cooperate, the Marshal would be informed, and the Nazis in his entourage would learn of the scheme and move troops into Tunisia, Morocco, and Algeria. As Weygand's prestige allegedly meant much in North Africa, FDR and the PM conceded that they were prepared to take that risk. Matthews was asked to take an oral message to Weygand via Ambassador Leahy in Vichy—as the United States still had fragile diplomatic relations with the Pétain regime—and Matthews had been Secretary at the Paris embassy when France fell. The scheme would not work, he argued. His presence would arouse the Gestapo. Besides, even though Weygand had been recalled from his North African command, he would not betray his colleagues. Roosevelt suggested his sending Weygand, whom he had known since 1918, a message couched subtly in terms of a Christmas or New Year's greeting—which he would do on December 27.

The conference broke up at noon so that Churchill could meet with representatives of the British and Empire press. He conceded that the situation in Malaya was dire and that Hong Kong was close to falling but that Britain had avoided "the worst possible situation"—being attacked by Japan alone, with America remaining out of the war. "On balance we could not be dissatisfied with the turn of events." With Russia "fighting back magnificently" and the "powerful assistance" of the United States to come, he looked ahead "with hope and confidence."

The first major conference of principal players, at 1:45 P.M., followed a quick vegetarian lunch (kedgeree and grilled tomatoes) at the White House. All the ranking conferees were present, plus Harry Hopkins and General "Pa" Watson as resident appointments secretary. General Marshall took notes. Roosevelt began by presenting a draft declaration "that no one power would

make peace without an agreement with the associate powers"—
the smaller nations already at war or plunged into the war. He reported agreement with Churchill on sending bombers and three
American divisions to Britain, withholding American troops
from the "Near East" (Egypt), and maintaining a "flying route"
across Africa via Brazil. The British vowed (perhaps with fingers
hidden and crossed) to "hold" Singapore while the United States
built up forces in Australia to assist "operations in the north including . . . the Philippines." With Churchill, the President assumed that Japan had unleashed all its offensive strength and
would not risk attacking Russia.

The Prime Minister conceded shortages in everything, from
munitions to manpower, and wanted the Americans to take over
Iceland from British forces to free them for deployment elsewhere. He thought that French North Africa was ripe for invasion unless the Germans got there first. The British could have
"55,000 men with transports ready for shipment for such a purpose and that they could be in Africa in twenty-three days." (It
was as unrealistic as his expectation that the British could hold
Singapore for half a year.) He suggested that if Vichy cooperated,
even passively, "the future France would be protected at the peace
table." Roosevelt added "that he considered it very important to
morale, to give this country a feeling that they are in the [Euro-
pean] war, to give the Germans the reverse effect, to have American troops somewhere in active fighting across the Atlantic." (He
had no idea how unready the United States was for concerted action anywhere, even had the catastrophe at Pearl Harbor not
happened.) Similarly unrealistic, as French malaise was profound,
Secretary Stimson "spoke of the importance of timing in relation
to movements into [Northern] Ireland and those projected for
the Mediterranean, with relation to its effect on the French people. He thought that our movement into Ireland would have a
very definite effect on the French mind, which would facilitate

53

arrangements for a movement into Tunisia and Morocco by the British and French." No one questioned his illogic. America was a new player.

Reviewing other fronts, Churchill warned that although the British presence in Libya and Egypt was precarious, "it would be a tremendous disaster to give up the [Suez] Canal—Turkey would go, Africa would be overrun." He suggested an expedition against Vichy French Dakar, on the hump of West Africa, to secure the air route from Brazil and as a jumping-off point for further operations. "I assume," Marshall questioned in his minutes, "this was on a basis of some agreement with the French." And Churchill again promised, in Marshall's notes, "Singapore to hold out. It ought to be a matter of six months before the Japanese can close in." (The "Gibraltar of the Pacific" would fall in six weeks, with more than a hundred thousand British and Empire troops taken prisoner—far greater than the Japanese forces in Malaya pushing south through deft strategy and defensive incompetence.)

At four o'clock, with the combined staff meeting temporarily adjourned, the President, wearing a grey pin-striped suit with a black mourning band on the left sleeve (his mother had died at eighty on September 10), was wheeled into the small, cluttered press room just inside the West Wing entrance to the White House. It would be his 794th press conference, this time with a guest at his side, attired now in short black jacket, striped trousers, and polka-dot bow tie. Cameramen stood on chairs to get a better shot of the Prime Minister, who was nearly a head shorter than FDR. The formal reason for the press's attendance was Roosevelt's announcement of the formation of the Office of Defense Transportation, but reporters expected Churchill to be there, and he was, sitting at FDR's right, a silver thermos of what was assumed to be water at his reach. As a record audience was filing in, press secretary Steve Early told the President, "They are checking credentials very carefully, and there are so many it is going to be slow."

Roosevelt repeated the message to the PM, joking, for the front rows, "We are afraid that there might be a wolf in sheep's clothing."

Churchill could barely be seen in the crowd. As newsmen shouted, "Can't see him," the President said to the PM, "I wish you would stand for one minute and let them see you. They can't see you." To loud cheers and applause from the journalists and broadcasters, Churchill, jaunty and ruddy, climbed on the seat of his chair.

Roosevelt cut his announcements to eight minutes, then noted, at Early's prompting, "There are many here who are not familiar with the rules of the conference, Steve says, and I would suggest that they remember that there are no 'quotes'—nothing is to be quoted. Everything is to be in the 'third person,' and can be used, with the exception of two matters. The Prime Minister doesn't know this [practice] himself. A thing that is 'background' may not be attributed to the President, or the Prime Minister, but it is for your information in writing stories. A thing that is announced as off-the-record is for your information, but not to be disclosed under any circumstances."

Then he turned the floor—literally the chair—to Churchill. "Go ahead and shoot," FDR told the reporters, and one began, "What about Singapore, Mr. Prime Minister? . . . What would you say to be of good cheer?" When the PM vowed that the British would do their utmost to defend Singapore "and its approaches," another pressman interposed, "Mr. Prime Minister, isn't Singapore "the key to the whole situation out there?"

"The key to whole situation," Churchill said, long accustomed to dodging direct questions in the House of Commons, "is the resolute manner in which the British and American Democracies

Franklin D. Roosevelt and Winston Churchill at their joint press conference in the president's White House office, December 23, 1941. *Franklin D. Roosevelt Presidential Library*

Close-up of Roosevelt and Churchill at joint press conference, December 23, 1941. *Franklin D. Roosevelt Presidential Library*

are going to throw themselves into the conflict." Conceding that the situation in the Far East looked gloomy, he could not contend that the war was turning round "in our favor." On balance, the PM said, "I can't describe the feelings of relief with which I find Russia, the United States and Great Britain standing side by side. It is incredible to anyone who has lived through the lonely months of 1940." Asked how long it would take to "lick these boys"—a demeaning cliché about the Japanese already catastrophically wrong, Churchill quipped, "If we manage it well, it will only take half as long as if we manage it badly."

"How long, sir, would it take if we managed it badly?"

"That has not been revealed to me at this moment. We don't have to manage it badly."

However clever the quips, the war was being managed badly, especially by Churchill himself, but the evidence would emerge slowly if at all before peace finally came. In Malaya, as earlier in the Mediterranean (especially in Greece), he was squandering resources to stave off inevitable humiliation.

Other questions ranged from the Eastern front (he saw the Germans as "joggling backwards" and praised Russian "resiliency") to plans afoot in Washington ("we have to concentrate on the grim emergencies") and to anticipations of new German initiatives. He foresaw a possible enemy "attack in the Mediterranean" and referred to "talk about their getting ready for an invasion of England next year." He thought something might come of it, but he could not predict where. "I will be glad to be informed. Gentlemen, if you have got any information, it will be thankfully received." What he received was laughter, and although a reporter thought that it seemed a closing remark and called out the ritual, "Thank you, Mr. Prime Minister," several other questions delayed the end. The last was, "What about a Christmas message for the American people?"

"I am told I have to do that on Christmas Eve," Churchill said, "but I won't give it away beforehand."

"The smiling President," *Newsweek* would report, "looked like an old trouper who, on turning impresario, had produced a smash hit. And some thought they detected in his face admiration for a man who had at least equaled him in the part in which he himself was a star."

As soon as pressmen rushed to typewriters, telephones, and microphones, Churchill slipped out to call Clementine in England. "He might have been speaking from the next room," she wrote to their daughter Mary the next day. "But it was not very satisfactory as it was a public line and we were both warned by the Censors breaking in that we were being listened to!" News of the press conference was furnished to Adolf Hitler by his propaganda minister, Joseph Goebbels. Hitler at dinner with his staff some days later described it "truly Jewish" theater produced by "imposters" who had deceived their nations. Goebbels was particularly pleased that war in the Pacific had created "a complete shift in the world picture. . . . The United States will scarcely now be in a position to transport worthwhile [war] materiel to England let alone the Soviet Union."

Hitler had not been so confident. As early as December 12, meeting with Grand Admiral Erich Raeder, he asked, "Is there any possibility that the U.S.A. and Britain will abandon East Asia for a time in order to crush Germany and Italy first?" Reassuringly, Raeder replied, "It is improbable that the enemy will give up East Asia even temporarily. By doing so Britain would endanger India very seriously, and the U.S. cannot withdraw her fleet from the Pacific as long as the Japanese fleet has the upper hand." Just in case, he added, he was ordering additional submarines to proceed "as quickly as possible" to the American east coast, where the lights had not yet dimmed. There was a different lighting problem in the east—in New

York City, where sixteen thousand traffic signals placed under central air-raid control disrupted traffic in Manhattan and Brooklyn during an alert. Police Commissioner Lewis Valentine forbade air-raid wardens to indulge in further tampering. The lights remained on.

ALTHOUGH THE LIBRARY OF CONGRESS was uninvolved in ongoing war planning, Archibald MacLeish, its director, a poet and occasional speechwriter for the President, had worried about the safety of the founding documents of the nation in his charge. After Pearl Harbor he inquired to Secretary of the Treasury Henry Morgenthau "whether space might be found at [the Bullion Depository in] Fort Knox for these materials, in the unlikely event that it becomes necessary to remove them from Washington." Morgenthau checked and allocated sixty cubic feet. Choices were made and procedures arranged and, sixteen days after war had broken out, MacLeish, with David C. Mearns, chief of the Manuscript Division, watched the preparations begin. "The documents were . . . wrapped," Mearns recalled, "in a container stiffened at top and bottom with all-rag, neutral millboard and secured by Scotch tape, and inserted in a specially-designed bronze container, which had been scrupulously cleaned of . . . possible harmful elements, and heated for six hours to a temperature of about 90°F to drive off any moisture. Empty space was then filled with sheets of all-rag, neutral millboard and the top of the container was screwed tight over a cork gasket and locked with padlocks on each side. It was late in the evening when work was suspended." In the sub-basement carpenter shop the container was placed in rock wool in a metal-bound box to await shipment after Christmas.

MUCH NEWS, like that episode, was withheld so that morale would not be affected by what looked like panic but was only prudence. An official censor had been appointed to monitor the release of news related to the war. He was Byron Price, fifty, the highly regarded executive news editor of the Associated Press, who was to control the media outside the government's own press bureaus and have no authority to "originate" news. Yet the army and navy could, and did. The navy sank subs that never existed, and MacArthur invented counterattacks that never happened.

Roosevelt and Churchill took a pass that evening, sharing drinks and dinner with Hopkins and a few household guests while the British and American staffs went to a dinner party for thirty-seven at the Carlton Hotel, hosted by Army Secretary Stimson and Navy Secretary Knox. Churchill delayed coming down, possibly because of telephone calls but perhaps also to forgo the President's mixed drinks in favor of brandy supplied by Alonzo Fields. With guests about at dinner, business was shelved for reminiscence, Roosevelt recalling his support of the Boers while he was at Harvard, while Churchill, in South Africa promoting the Empire, was taken prisoner and, on escaping, earning acclaim at home. After Roosevelt added that schooling did not bring back many pleasant memories, Churchill put down his cigar and agreed. "When I hear a man say that his childhood was the happiest time of his life, I think, my friend, you have had a pretty poor life."

At the Carlton Hotel Stimson opened with a toast to George VI, which was responded to by Admiral Sir Dudley Pound's toast to the President. At the close, Stimson, an artillery colonel in the earlier war, noted in his diary, "I recalled my recollections of 1917 when America had just declared war and a British mission for a similar purpose had crossed the ocean and came to us." Now, he said, "twenty-four years afterwards the same situation was presenting itself, the same hope and ideal lay before us, and this time we must not fail, but must win the war and the peace."

After dinner they gathered in an adjoining room, Stimson recalled, "and chatted over our problems. There was a very hearty spirit of cooperation and good will evidenced on both sides and not a single note, so far as I could see, intervened to mar the earnest spirit of harmony and endeavor which pervaded everybody." Churchill cabled to his Deputy Prime Minister Clement Attlee, the Labour Party leader, "We live here as a big family in the greatest intimacy and informality, and I have formed the very highest regard for the President. His breadth of view, resolution and his loyalty to the common cause are beyond all praise."

Roosevelt may have retired early after his long dinner with the PM and Hopkins, but it is likely that Hopkins and Churchill, with rooms across the hallway from each other, talked shop into the morning, stimulated not only by events but by the spirits, however different, both could not do without. Hopkins, often disabled by internal troubles requiring drastic surgery, persisted heroically through them and the war as the President's legs, but as he lay dying soon after, would write from his hospital bed to Robert Sherwood, who assisted in writing Roosevelt's speeches, that his doctors "are struggling over a very bad case of cirrhosis of the liver—not due, I regret to say, from taking too much alcohol. . . . I dislike hating the effect of a long life of congenial and useful drinking and neither deserve the reputation nor enjoy its pleasures."

Across the continent in Seattle, someone after dark sounded a fire alarm and a wannabe Paul Revere on horseback galloped about the city shouting, "Blackout! Air raid! The Jap bombers are coming!" Ostensibly to enforce the false alarm, mobs plunged about the downtown area smashing neon signs and lighted shop windows, looting the displays. Scenes like it occurred elsewhere, but mostly in the west. There, panic was easiest to stir, military aircraft punctuated the skies, and Christmas merchandise loomed invitingly behind glass. None of the "strange planes" were strange.

December 24, 1941
Christmas Eve

O N T H E *Nagato* at ten—it was X + 16, X being the opening day of the war—the chief of the naval general staff, Admiral Osami Nagano, boarded to offer a battle report about Pearl Harbor, based on interviews with the returned crews, now anchored at Kure. Although still morning, the presentation was followed, Admiral Ugaki wrote, "by a drinking party." Then the brass left for the *Akagi*, flagship of the Pearl Harbor strike force, where Admiral Yamamoto spoke to commanders and officers of *Kido Butai*. "Pictures were taken and toasts followed."

In Surabaja, once the crews of the *Pope* and *Ford* were paid at one-and-a-half Dutch guilders to the dollar, they were granted Christmas Eve liberty. Many put on their whites and took tenders ashore. According to the *Ford*'s diary, Mac McKean, Dan Nowlin, R. M. Soyars and Henry Mate

caught a Dutch Navy bus into town and had no trouble in finding a nice combination restaurant and bar. Someone there knew a little English and was helpful in the choice of food. Heinekens beer was recognized immediately and ordered. Then McKean spotted a glass enclosed counter with lots of rich, creamy cakes and cookies of various sizes and shapes. They ate like food was going out of style and everyone enjoyed their enthusiasm. There was no order in their eating and drinking. Beer mixed with the rich cakes and the entré[e], then more beer before and after dessert, and more beer. There were girls, too—who were easy to talk to, even if each did not understand the other, at first. After a couple of hours of vocabulary swapping and sign language, none had any difficulty understanding the other.

Jon Cross, William Mack, and C. A. Darrah of *Ford* were also in the first boat ashore. "They caught a cab to the Dutch Naval Officer's Club, a prestigious large clubhouse on the outskirts of town. It was one fancy place, with silver place settings, flowers, immaculate adornments, etc. They stayed at the bar and sampled several curry appetizers, but noticing that most of the tables were reserved, they left for the Hotel Oranje. There they had a marvelous Xmas dinner,* followed by several fancy drinks. Truely a relaxing time after weeks at sea, with its deprivation, privation, and just gut-tightening watch standing and alerts."

The account was understated. All the ships that had made it to Java had left behind dead and wounded at Cavite, and many of the bomb-damaged ships and their crews would not survive beyond Darwin, Australia. Balikpapan would fall to the Japanese on January 24, barely a month later, and exotic Surabaja would fall on March 4, with much of its trapped Dutch and mixed-race population destined at best for bleak prison camps and near-starvation.

---

*According to the menu kept by one of the group: lobster, oxtail soup, medallions of veal, roast goose with chestnuts, Christmas pudding, "Glace Surprises de Noël," and "Corbeille de Fruits," followed by coffee.

CHRISTMAS EVE IN THE PHILIPPINES, to the southeast and an hour before Tokyo time, came more than half a day earlier than in the United States, across the International Date Line. The nearly unopposed Japanese landing at Lamon Bay, southeast of Manila, that morning had left the capital defenseless from every direction. Based on MacArthur's communiqués, largely fiction, the *New York Times* headlined, "OUR TANKS AND ARTILLERY POUND INVADERS." Landing at Lingayen Gulf and quickly moving south, General Homma set up his headquarters north of San Fernando, above Manila Bay. Not far below, defenders were protecting the Calumpit Bridges, over which they funneled retreating troops, and failed to prevent refugees from fleeing, into the Bataan Peninsula, a two hundred–square mile thumb of hills and jungle thrusting south into Manila Bay. Much of Luzon's stored food supplies for defending troops were now beyond reach. Major General Jonathan Wainwright put soldiers on two-thirds rations. His forces were already backing into Bataan where, according to MacArthur's Plan Orange 3, they were to hold on for six months until relief would come from the American mainland. But by every measure Orange had become instantly obsolete on the first day of the war. His radioed proposal that such fleet units from Hawaii as were left should risk an attack on the Japanese Home Islands in order to draw enemy strength away from the Southwest Pacific was considered fantasy by Washington, as was his proposal that the only two big carriers in the Pacific could fly aircraft to the Philippines.

That afternoon MacArthur's deputy, Brigadier General Richard Sutherland, summoned key officers to headquarters in Intramuros to inform them that they would be leaving Manila for Corregidor at dusk. MacArthur took a last glance at his flag-bedecked office and asked Sergeant Paul Rogers to "cut off" the red banner with the four white stars of a full general which flew from the limousine he would have to abandon. Rogers untied the thongs from the post and rolled up the flag. MacArthur thanked him, tucked it under his arm, and crossed palm-lined Dewey (now Roxas) Boulevard to the Manila Hotel.

Each staff member would be permitted field equipment and one suitcase or bedroll. Jean MacArthur again unwrapped her presents and filled her suitcase (labeled New Grand Hotel, Yokohama) and that of her son and his *amah*, Ah Cheu, with clothes, canned food, her jewelry, some family pictures, her husband's medals wrapped in a towel monogrammed Manila Hotel, and his gold Philippines army field marshal's baton. Sid Huff carried Arthur's new tricycle, and Ah Cheu his stuffed rabbit, Old Friend. Before departing Intramuros, MacArthur had sent for Japanese Consul-General Nihro Katsumi, then in mild detention, to ask him to confirm to the Japanese command that defenseless Manila was to be declared an Open City.

"Ready to go to Corregidor, Arthur?" Jean MacArthur asked the bewildered boy. He nodded and took Ah Cheu's hand as she opened the door to the wail of air-raid sirens. The MacArthurs, with Huff, left for the Cavite docks in the general's black Packard. The extensive military history library, and everything else in the flat, would be at the pleasure of General Homma.

At 7:00 P.M. the interisland steamer *Don Esteban* weighed anchor for Corregidor with the MacArthur party aboard. After dark it was still a warm eighty degrees, and some of those who had gone below crowded onto the forward deck for the breezes stirred by the passage. In the quiet of evening, with enemy aircraft gone and the glow of the fires on the Cavite docks receding, a few, unwilling to miss Christmas altogether, began singing "Silent Night"—and others joined in with further carols until they felt too depressed to continue. (Biographer William Manchester wrote, rather, that no one joined a lone caroler.) There was nothing to encourage evacuees to believe that Corregidor and Bataan could hold out until rescue. The huge, squat mortars which were the Rock's most formidable defensive weapons were embossed "Bethlehem Steel. 1898."

Philippines President Manuel Quezon, a tubercular with a hacking cough, had left Manila earlier, unrecognized in an American army uniform and steel helmet. Parting with his loyal executive secretary Jorge Vargas, Quezon instructed him to wait in Manila for the Japanese and secure the best deal for the city he could. "You have my absolute confidence, and I am sure you will not fail me." On orders, Vargas was to cooperate with the occupation short only of taking an oath of allegiance to the Japanese Empire.

"Mr. President," said Vargas, "no matter what happens, you can count on me, whether in Malakanyang [Palace] if the Japanese allow me to remain, or in my house in Kawilihan."

General Douglas MacArthur and ailing President Manuel Quezon, who had been evacuated from Manila. *Courtesy MacArthur Memorial Library & Archives*

Two launches took Quezon's party to the *Mayon,* almost a mile out in the bay, now delayed in departure because the ship's chief engineer had gone back into Manila to pack his clothes. Impatient and worried about new raids on the harbor, Quezon ordered the *Mayon*'s crew to sail with or without the absent engineer. Vincente Madrigal, the shipowner, ordered the third engineer to fire the engines, and the ship soon lifted anchor. By dusk Quezon was at the Corregidor pier saluted by a Filipino guard of honor. But the guard of honor had a more urgent purpose. Quezon had not needed much urging from MacArthur to order truckloads of crated gold and silver bullion from the Philippines treasury rushed under heavy guard to dockside for storage in a Corregidor tunnel.

Outside military and government offices in the city, bonfires of papers from abandoned files were still burning. On the waterfront at Cavite, oil storage tanks, put to the torch, spewed heavy black smoke into the night. What was left of the navy, but for three gunboats, six PT boats, and Admiral Hart's submarines, set off after dark for Java. A few patched-up P-40 fighters had been flown to Corregidor's postage-stamp Kindley Field. On departure MacArthur handed Carlos Romulo, his Philippine assistant for press relations, a sealed envelope—the Open City declaration for Manila.

Blacked-out Corregidor was only thirty miles from the mainland at Cavite, but before the *Don Esteban* reached the island's North Dock, little Arthur announced that he was tired and wanted to go home. Home, however, would be Corregidor, where Major General George Moore, the commandant, greeted the MacArthurs and escorted them toward cots in a tunnel. MacArthur announced that he would not live in a dank tunnel. "Where are *your* quarters?" he asked. At Topside, said Moore. (There was also Middleside and Bottomside, identifying the heights of the Rock.) "We'll move in there tomorrow morning," said his superior. But the house is exposed to air attacks, Moore warned. "That's fine," said MacArthur. "Just the thing." Neither the house nor the arrangement would last very long.

No churchgoer in any denomination, although he often quoted Scripture in his speeches and proclamations, MacArthur did not attend midnight Christmas Mass. Open to Filipinos as well as Americans, it was celebrated by Catholic service chaplains in the Malinta Tunnel, which penetrated the Rock.

⸙

"I RECEIVED WORD THIS MORNING," Stimson wrote, wondering when if ever the Prime Minister slept, "that Churchill was anxious for a talk with me on the subject of the Philippines, so I spent the first part of the morning preparing for that besides attending to my other administrative work. I then went over to the White House with [Brigadier] General Eisenhower of the War Plans Division to back me up in case I was asked questions that I couldn't answer." Churchill had already improvised the map room near his bedroom, where the three talked about the Philippines. The morning papers had reported that the Japanese had landed a "strong force" by forty troopships south of Manila and were already closing in on the capital from Lingayen Gulf to the north. The Lamon Bay force, landing at the narrow neck of central Luzon, numbered only eight thousand, far inferior except in desire from MacArthur's US and Filipino troops who, the general had reported dramatically, were standing off the enemy "against great odds." In actuality they were withdrawing, north and south, toward Bataan. Supplies that might have been prudently stockpiled earlier on "the Rock" were abandoned, including those dockside at Cavite. Tokyo Radio described the ongoing retreat into Bataan as "a cat entering a sack."

———— ⟨≋⟩ ————

ROMINTEN, a heath in East Prussia that was a favorite hunting ground for *Reichsmarschall* Hermann Göring, was close to Hitler's headquarters and as close to the Russian front as Göring was likely to venture. His air commander on the Eastern Front, Colonel-General Wolfram von Richthofen, came to ask permission to have *Luftwaffe* troops unneeded in the winter weather made available for infantry duty. "They must fight, win, or die where they stand," Göring insisted, accusing him of "whining." Nevertheless he went with Richthofen from "Robinson," the curiously christened air force forward headquarters nearby, to *Wolfsschanze* to let the general make the same case to Hitler. "The *Reichsmarschall* and I were very persuasive," von Richthofen noted in his diary. "*Führer* swears loudly about the army commanders responsible for much of this mess." Warily, Göring visited Hitler only once more during the winter, on December 27. Otherwise he remained at his vast Prussian estate, "Carinhall," bursting with art treasures looted from Holland, France, and other occupied countries. "For days now the *Reichsmarschall* has vanished," General Hoffmann von Waldau, the deputy air chief, wrote from "Robinson" on Christmas Eve. "*He* gets to spend Christmas at home. It's important to set an example in little things. We are going to have to get used to harder times." Yet Waldau himself would venture no farther forward than East Prussia.

———— ⟨≋⟩ ————

ABOARD THE *Regnbue,* with the convoy still roughly in formation, chatter abounded about Christmas Eve dinner for the crew, its scheduled time changing as they moved westward across the time zones. "Rumors," A. J. Liebling wrote, "were spread by one of the British machine gunners, who had talked to the third engineer, who had it straight from a messboy, that there would be turkey. While the convoy moved along at its steady ten knots, nobody aboard the *Regnbue* talked of anything but the coming dinner." On the great night the captain's table in the saloon was laid for a dozen places—officers, the radioman, a gunner, and Liebling. To mark the occasion, as there were no alarms about subs or planes and the sea was still calm, the officers wore neckties. Engineer Larsen raised a glass of gin and pronounced "Skoal!" Then came a thick soup with canned shrimp and crabmeat, after it fish pudding. The turkey was brought in ceremoniously by the steward "with the pride of a Soviet explorer presenting a hunk of frozen mammoth excavated from a glacier."

Between each course were further skoals, in which the teetotaler Methodist captain did not join. Willem Petersen "brought out a couple of songbooks that he had got from a Norwegian church and suggested we sing some Christmas hymns," duly done "without much pleasure," following which they ate mounds of doughnuts and "a lot of jello covered with vanilla sauce" and drank more gin. Feeling awkward after the hymns, the men's faces remained rigid and solemn until the steward brought in triple portions of gin with lump sugar and cherries. Whiskey was served straight as a dessert liquor. The men sang Norwegian folk songs between skoals until the captain asked "our American friend" to sing a song from his own country—"My Old Kentucky Home." Liebling knew few of the words, especially after all the "yin," but happily three crewmen began singing three different Norwegian songs at the same time. Then others drifted in from their dinner groups, all now unable to appear Christmas-solemn—"first the argumentative carpenter, then the boatswain with the cackle, and finally the pumpman, a tall fellow who looked like a Hapsburg and spent his life shooting compressed air into clogged oil tanks."

Men began leaving their tables to stand—if they could—their watches. Announcing, "I am a Commoonist, so I want you to love these fellers," the steward handed out bottles of Old Angus whiskey and Christmas greetings from the Norwegian government-in-exile, each with the facsimile signature, "Haakon, Rex." The crewmen aft were all wearing blue stocking caps which had come to dockside in a Christmas gift package with cards identifying the Santa headgear as having been knitted by Miss Georgie Gunn of 1035 Park Avenue, New York City.

ONCE THE PRESIDENT had awakened, Eleanor hung a Christmas stocking on the mantel in his bedroom for Fala, with rubber bones and other chewable toys. Diana Hopkins had a stocking hung at the fireplace in her father's bedroom. She was the only resident child in the White House. For FDR and for Hopkins Mrs. Roosevelt had bought and packaged bed capes in Christmas paper. Her husband's was a navy-blue wool wrap-around with his initials embroidered in red. A deluge of Christmas presents and greeting cards had already been arriving at the White House and at the British Embassy for Churchill, and would continue all week. Box after box of cigars would be posted to the PM, eight thousand cigars in all. Bottles of vintage brandy; gloves, socks and scarves; a box of fresh onions; catnip for the Churchill cat at Chequers; and the inevitable religious tracts. As no one could examine every one of the gifts to determine which may have concealed explosives or poison, for security reasons the Secret Service ruled that only Christmas gifts for the Prime Minister from persons identified and specially cleared could be accepted.

Churchill "was still in deshabille, wearing a sort of zipper pajama suit and slippers," Stimson wrote. "I had brought maps of

Franklin D. Roosevelt in his study with Fala, December 1941. *Franklin D. Roosevelt Presidential Library*

the Philippines and explained the location of the different troops on both sides, the course of the campaign, and its probable outcome in a retreat to Corregidor. Eisenhower [who probably did the explaining] then retired and I had a further talk with [Churchill] about other matters. . . . He explained to me particularly his views on the West African problem." Churchill wanted a quick takeover of Vichy French Africa, and much of the meetings into January would deal with its attractions—and impossibility.

The military chiefs and their staffs convened at 10:30 A.M. in the imposing marble Federal Reserve Building near the War and Navy departments, taking up points in order of assumed priority. Admiral Harold ("Betty") Stark began by declaring that the British Isles were to be protected "at all cost." Island defenses needed more deterrent capacity, as invasion remained a possibility as long as the Germans held the Channel ports in France. Field Marshal Dill responded that the defenses were "constantly being improved." When Stark noted that American heavy bombers to be sent to Britain would be manned by American crews, Air Marshal Portal objected that it was not part of the original agreement. He saw inexperienced American airmen as a burden, even if experiencing the real thing would make them useful. Stark explained that those planes with their crews would supplement aircraft to be supplied for British use, and General Marshall reminded Portal that the PM himself had noted how important externally a visible American presence would be, including the American divisions which would also be assigned, subject to "the availability of tonnage."

The conferees discussed the relief of British troops in Iceland, and General Gerow advised that the changeover could be completed by March—but again, everything hinged on shipping and the havoc wrought by German subs in the North Atlantic. More patrols were needed, said Stark. "We just don't have any destroyers to spare, and in fact have fewer for our own needs." Like Iceland, Greenland would be a staging area for air transport, General Arnold added. One field was ready and another was being prepared. When North Africa again came up, Marshall observed that "a token [American] force as part of the British forces would be feasible, but he could not [safely] put a lone regiment on the coast of Africa." Obviously Vichy French Africa remained a target many months away.

When the conferees turned to the Pacific Rim, Field Marshal Dill suggested that "with reinforcements, the British would be able to hold Johore State," on the Kra Peninsula above Singapore. No one disputed him. (Reinforcements would continue to arrive, as late as February 5, little more than a week before the abject surrender.) General Arnold was asked about the possibility of bombing Japan from unoccupied China. There was no point in it, he said, unless American air power was "strong enough to create substantial damage. . . . Unsustained attacks would only tend to solidify the Japanese people." (Within weeks his views about a token operation would change, leading to the daring Doolittle raid in April and its likely impact in June on the climactic battle off Midway Island.) The aircraft carrier situation, Stark advised, was "very bad, and that . . . the Navy was making plans to convert passenger ships and tankers into airplane carriers." Twenty other matters were discussed, but the four Churchill/Chiefs of Staff memoranda were deferred for further study, and the meeting adjourned for a late lunch.

Churchill knew that he had a Christmas Eve speech to deliver at the White House tree lighting and worked on it between compulsive trips to his Monroe Room map center. Red dispatch boxes were constantly arriving from the Embassy, and further reports from the President's staff. Promising news came from Russia, where the German drives on Moscow and besieged and desperate Leningrad were stalled, and from Libya, where Axis forces were retreating from Benghazi and heading for Tripoli while waiting for air and land reinforcements from Russia, where winter had made them of little use. Elsewhere the Japanese were pushing into Burma, endangering the supply route north into China, and moving southward against little resistance in Malaya. Hong Kong was near surrender, trapping Canadian troops sent there by Churchill belatedly and sacrificially, and the Netherlands Indies were being penetrated at multiple points, with little hope, despite the dwindling Dutch navy, to save any of the islands. The PM moved his pins about.

Determined not to be without his own map room, the President ordered one created, and Lieutenant Robert Montgomery of Naval Intelligence, a reservist out of Hollywood for the duration, was assigned to the job. Space was limited; toilets and sinks were removed from a ladies' cloakroom in the basement, as

"Lighting up." Churchill and Roosevelt in conference with their iconic cigar and cigarette in long holder. *Cartoon from Vineland, NJ,* Journal, *January 5, 1942.*

Montgomery superintended the conversion of a ladies' cloak-room in the basement into a secure information center, staffed by a joint Army-Navy team under Captain John McCrea, a new naval aide to the President. The Army Signal Corps would run it as a heavily guarded message center, accessible to Roosevelt, Hopkins, and senior military personnel. Montgomery supplemented the color-coded pins on the fiberboard-mounted maps, with special ones for special people. FDR's was a cigarette holder, Churchill's a cigar. Stalin was represented by a briar pipe. Franklin Jr.'s destroyer was coded, as well as capital ships. See-through plastic sheets covered land operations, their battle lines changed with a grease pencil. Guam was marked as lost, and other pins confirmed worsening news not yet in newspapers.

While working committees met indoors, preparations were being completed for the annual lighting of the outdoor White House ("National Community") Christmas tree. For Roosevelt,

Christmas trees were more than symbols. He raised them for revenue at Hyde Park, listing his occupation on his voting registration form as "tree farmer." The "planting and the raising and the selling of Christmas trees," he would tell a press and radio conference, was "close to my heart." He once thought of making "a radio speech" on the subject, he confessed.

> I have some very, very carefully kept books on the subject of Christmas trees—a thing called a check-book. And I pay for the labor of planting these little trees at the age of four years and about six inches high, and I pay a man—oh—about every two years—to go through and keep the briars out of them; and then I pay several people—some of them schoolboys—to go in and cut them off. . . . Along comes a department store or chain store with a truck, and they themselves load these little trees—this is ten years after the planting—into the truck. They take them down to New York, and sell the trees—at a profit. . . . And then they send me a check.

Prior to each holiday season, his secretary, Grace Tully, recalled, she would write to "one of the chain stores, . . . reminding them that the President had trees for sale," and the stores "would buy the entire year's output. . . . He only made a small profit but he hoped one day to produce trees in such quantity that it would be really a profitable venture."

For security in wartime the Secret Service proposed to have the formidable national Christmas tree, much too tall to be a Hyde Park product, erected in Lafayette Park, a seven-acre expanse across Pennsylvania Avenue from the White House, as the event would draw thousands of unidentifiable persons. The President insisted that tradition required the White House lawn. Within the patrolled iron-picket fence around the White House grounds, only those specifically invited would get close to the participants on the South Portico. Even so, guards warned, "No cameras, no packages." A tent outside the two gates had been set up as a package checking station, but some visitors refused to give up their places in line at the four o'clock opening and dropped their Christmas bundles at the fence, hoping they would find them again afterward. The uninvited could watch from beyond—and under a crescent moon thousands were already gathering in the early winter twilight.

Was a brilliantly lit hazard being created at odds with unenforced wartime brownouts? The White House was assured that no enemy could penetrate Washington airspace. Also, Christmas Eve traditions were exempted in the interest of national confidence. Despite restrictions involving landmarks, the red aircraft-warning light 550 feet atop the Washington Monument remained aglow and could be seen from the White House lawn. At the lighting ceremonies in 1940, realizing that war was approaching from somewhere, and perhaps soon, the President had told the crowd that it was welcome to return in 1941 "if we are all still here." Many were back.

Christmas Eve 1941 was the only public occasion when Roosevelt and Churchill spoke from the same platform. As they gathered with guests and the White House staff in the East Room an hour before the ceremonies at five, the Marine Band on the South Lawn struck up holiday music, beginning with "Joy to the World," accompanied by choirs from nearby churches. Outranking the Prime Minister in the party were stately, beautiful Crown Princess Marthe of occupied Norway and her princely husband, the future King Olav V.* Marthe, whom FDR adored,

---

*Forty in 1941, Marthe had become First Lady of Norway when her mother-in-law, Queen Maud, died in 1938. Her husband spent much of his time with the government-in-exile in London. The crown princess would never become queen. Marthe died in 1954.

was one of the rare women he kissed whenever they met. With her children, she had been offered a temporary White House residence after fleeing Norway, until she could find an American home, which she did nearby in Maryland. In what seemed like a royal gesture, each White House employee was presented with a signed photograph of Franklin and Eleanor.

When the sunset gun at Fort Myer, across the Potomac, boomed, the band began "Hail to the Chief," and the President, on the arm of an aide, was escorted slowly out to the south balcony with Mrs. Roosevelt and the Prime Minister. Following them, the White House party, many shivering in the chill evening, watched as FDR pressed a button lighting the big evergreen at the lower slope of the lawn. The crowd applauded, their eyes especially on Churchill. Then the Rev. Joseph Corrigan, rector of Catholic University in northeast Washington, delivered a brief invocation tailored to the times. "Hear an united people, girded for battle" he began, looking up, "dedicate themselves to the peace of Christmas." He confessed "strangeness" in such a contradiction in words, yet "All the material resources with which Thou has blessed our native land, we consecrate to the dread tasks of war." It was what Churchill wanted to hear and the reason he had come.

Radio carried their voices across the country and abroad. As the Christmas lights glowed, Roosevelt spoke directly to the event. "It is in the spirit of peace and good will, and with particular thoughtfulness of those, our sons and brothers, who serve in our armed forces on land and sea, near and far—those who serve and endure for us—that we light our Christmas candles now across this continent from one coast to the other on this Christmas evening."

Now, he added, "my associate, my old and good friend" wanted to speak to Washingtonians and to the world. No one in hearing distance had any doubt as to who that was, especially once his

President Roosevelt (with Prime Minister Churchill behind him) on the White House portico lighting the White House Christmas tree. *Franklin D. Roosevelt Presidential Library*

rolling, almost antique, voice echoed across the lights and shadows. "This is a strange Christmas eve," Churchill began:

> Almost the whole world is locked in deadly struggle, and with the most terrible weapons which science can devise, the nations advance upon each other. Ill would it be for us this Christmastide if we were not sure that no greed for the land or wealth of any other people, no vulgar ambition, no morbid lust for material gain at the expense of others has led us to the field. Here, in the midst of war, raging and soaring over all the lands and seas, creeping nearer to our hearts and our homes, here, amid the tumult, we have tonight the peace of the spirit in each cottage home and in each generous heart. There, we may cast aside for

this night at least the cares and dangers which beset us, and make for our children an evening of happiness in a world of storm. Here, then, for one night only, each home throughout the English-speaking world should be a brightly lighted island of happiness and peace.

While far from his own hearth and family, he continued, "Yet I cannot truthfully say that I feel far from home." He referred to his kinship with his audiences, listening rapt on the White House lawn, and nationwide:

Whether it be ties of blood on my mother's side, or the friendships I have developed here over many years of active life, or the commanding sentiment of comradeship in the common cause of great peoples who speak the same language, who kneel at the same altars, and, to a very large extent, pursue the same ideals, I cannot feel myself a stranger here at the centre and at the summit of the United States. I feel a sense of unity and fraternal association which, added to the kindliness of your welcome, convinces me that I have a right to sit at your fireside and share your Christmas joys.

It was, he conceded, "a strange Christmas eve," with war "raging and roaring over all the lands and seas, creeping nearer to our hearts and homes." Nevertheless, the PM concluded, using the English equivalent for Santa,

Let the children have their night of fun and laughter. Let the gifts of Father Christmas delight their play. Let us grown-ups share to the full in their unstinted pleasures before we turn again to the stern task and the formidable years that lie before us, resolved that by our sacrifice and daring, these same children shall not be robbed of their inheritance or denied their right to live in a free and decent world.

And so, in God's mercy, a happy Christmas to you all.

Not knowing whether to cheer or remain in reverent silence, the crowd registered a mélange of emotions. The presidential party withdrew indoors, and the thousands on the lawn and beyond moved toward Pennsylvania Avenue, some seeking, in the darkness, their safeguarded Christmas packages. Waiting trolley cars, their interior lights pale yellow, many drawn out of retirement to replace buses gone into military service, waited. Soon the lights on the tall evergreen cast shadows on White House grounds that had emptied.

As on the evening before, guests reassembled in the Red Room, the President and PM arriving late after conferring briefly with Secretary Knox, Admiral Pound, and Brigadier (General) Leslie Hollis to discuss emergency needs as the situation in Malaya and the Philippines continued to deteriorate. Roosevelt agreed to permit a British brigade embarked on the American transport *Mount Vernon* for Colombo, Ceylon, to proceed instead to Singapore. With Australia already endangered, Army Air Forces general George H. Brett, then in China, was ordered to proceed Down Under to take charge of aircraft and crews to be ferried there or were already lengthily en route via Africa and India. All the carrying capacity of available shipping was in use. Because heavy bombers could somehow, with refueling stops, fly to Australia, Brett was to establish a subcommand only nominally under MacArthur, with "action to be taken in view of situation in Philippines at that time [of arrival]." The radioed message was signed "Marshall," but that meant Eisenhower.

Better news had come from Libya, where General Claude Auchinleck's forces were advancing. An "Enigma" decrypt had already revealed that German panzers were withdrawing, and that afternoon Auchinleck had telegraphed, "Royal Dragoons occupied Benghazi this morning. The Army of the Nile sends you hearty greetings for Christmas." (The euphoria would not last. Its supply lines overextended and the Germans resupplied by air, the Eighth Army would be driven back early in 1942.)

At Christmas 1940 the White House had throbbed with a noisy gathering of Roosevelt grandchildren. Now, given the lack of family and the preponderance of unusual guests, the President planned to forgo a family tradition going back to the childhoods of his five children, four of them (but for Anna, his only daughter) now away at war. He would not read aloud, very likely to Eleanor's relief, Charles Dickens's *A Christmas Carol,* in which, annually, he had taken all the roles in different voices.

In the Red Room Crown Prince Olav, with Marthe, and the British guests—Churchill, Wilson, and Beaverbrook—shared predinner drinks with the Roosevelts, an hour marred by Eleanor's reminding her husband that he had not telephoned holiday greetings to Missy LeHand, FDR's secretary and confidant over two decades, with him even before Roosevelt's paralysis. Marguerite LeHand had been invalided by a stroke in June 1940. He confessed that it had escaped him. "The sudden influx and the increasing work made it practically impossible for him to think too much about any personal sorrow," Mrs. Roosevelt would write, explaining that it was their first Christmas without her imperious mother-in-law, Sara, who had died in September at eighty-six. But Eleanor was peeved that he brushed aside calling Missy, who in some ways had taken over the First Lady's own role with the President. (What seemed like callousness to Eleanor was her husband's almost total detachment from formerly close relationships once their usefulness had passed.) When Marguerite's sister, Ann Rochon, wrote to Mrs. Roosevelt after a visit to Warm Springs that Missy had enjoyed "all the

Roosevelt and Churchill at Christmas dinner in the White House.
Franklin D. Roosevelt Presidential Library

wonderful Christmas presents" received from the White House, very likely it was the first that FDR knew about them.

Informal Christmas dinner conversation at the White House got around, inevitably, to food, Percy Chubb recalled. Chubb, a marine insurance executive, had known the Roosevelts since FDR had been assistant secretary of the Navy in the earlier war. The food supplies being shipped to Britain, Churchill had commented only half-seriously, included "too many powdered eggs. The only good thing you can make with them is Spotted Dick." (The traditional steamed English pudding was made with raisins and currants—the spots—in a dough of suet, eggs, and flour.)

"Nonsense," said the President. "You can do as much with a powdered egg as with a real egg."

"I opened my mouth for the only time all evening," Chubb recalled, "to ask how you could fry a powdered egg."

December 25, 1941
Christmas Day

THE JAPANESE HAD CLAIMED to have taken Midway in the first days of the Pacific war, but the three-segment coral atoll, little more than a refueling stop in peacetime for amphibious Yankee Clippers en route to Manila, had held off landing attempts and repeated bombardments. At 11:40 P.M., anticipating the holiday on his side of the Date Line, a Midway serviceman at the communications shack, after a long silence from the island, radioed the *New York Times* news desk cheerily: "We are still here. Merry Christmas."

At Wake Island, to the east of the Date Line, more than fifteen hundred military and civilian-contractor survivors, excluding a few dozen officers kept separately, squatted on the shell-pocked airfield runway, two hundred feet wide, in sun and then rain, where they had been herded since surrender, many first bound with telephone wire. For Christmas they were each given a bowl of thin rice gruel. In the United States the dispiriting but misleading headlines made the newspapers on Christmas Day. According to the *Dallas Morning News,*

In a cartoon by Ralph Lee, a battered but defiant Marine on Wake Island, December 1941, shakes his fist angrily at Japanese planes overhead. *Department of Defense, USMC*

DOFF YOUR HATS, U.S.,
TO MARINES ON WAKE!
Fighting Huge Odds, 385 of Them
Give Japs Hell for Fourteen Days

There had been 388 marines in the detachment on the atoll, plus bluejackets, aircraft mechanics, VMF-211 Hellcat pilots, and medical staff—522 in all—and 1,146 Morrison-Knudsen Company employees. Forty-nine marines and navy men had died as well as sixty-five construction workers, many fighting with whatever weapons were available. More would be executed on Wake, die aboard ships to Shanghai and to Japan, and in prison camps, often near coal mines where they were forced to work.

AMID HEAVY GROUND FIGHTING and bombardment on Christmas morning near incongruously named Happy Valley in Hong Kong, artillery sergeant Charles Barman's battery, about to withdraw further, received a radio message from Royal Governor Sir Mark Young:

> IN PRIDE AND ADMIRATION, I SEND MY GREETINGS THIS CHRISTMAS DAY TO ALL WHO ARE FIGHTING AND TO ALL WHO ARE WORKING SO NOBLY AND SO WELL TO SUSTAIN HONG KONG AGAINST THIS ASSAULT BY THE ENEMY. FIGHT ON, HOLD FAST FOR KING, COUNTRY AND EMPIRE. GOD BLESS YOU ALL IN THIS FINEST HOUR.

Christmas Day in the British army in more serene times was given over to light-hearted reversal of the traditional norms. Sergeants took early morning tea to the ranks, still in bed, and officers waited on them at table. It was an interlude of uninhibited fraternization, football matches, and jolly intemperance. In Hong Kong more than half the island had been overrun, and the defenders were still grudgingly giving way—nearly sleepless Middlesexers, Scots, Canadians, Australians, Rajputs, and Punjabis—reduced to a few light machine guns, rifles, and hand grenades. All were on nearly depleted short rations of food and water. A Red Cross flag on the War Memorial Hospital, where a group of Winnipeg Grenadiers were offered tots of whiskey and a routine "Merry Christmas!" by Lieutenant Colonel George Black, MD, a sixtyish veteran of the earlier war, furnished no respite from shelling. Soon the wounded were being bayoneted in their beds.

The last radio message from abroad before communications failed had been from the Prime Minister to Sir Mark Young. Empty of reality and heedless of the human cost, it directed that "the enemy should be compelled to expend the utmost life and equipment. . . . Every day that you are able to maintain your resistance you help the Allied cause all over the world, and by a prolonged resistance you and your men can win the lasting honour which we are sure will be your due."

What early Christmas dinner Sir Mark was served in shelled Government House is unrecorded. His military commander, Major General Charles Maltby, with his aide, Lieutenant MacGregor, sat on upturned ammunition boxes and shared a tin of asparagus and a half-bottle of lukewarm Liebfraumilch. Others on the staff opened tins of bully-beef and biscuits, and beer, pickled onions, and cognac—anything that was left. At 3:15 P.M.— early morning in Washington—General Maltby, informed that the situation everywhere was "damned sticky," issued orders to break off fighting. Early that evening he and Sir Mark surrendered the remnants of their forces—and the island—to Lieutenant General Sakai. About four thousand defenders had died and nine thousand were wounded. Thousands more, soldier and civilian, would die in grim prisoner of war camps.

"The report of the fall of Hong Kong came," Admiral Ugaki noted. "It seemed that they had a hard fight with the English troops who defended well. Indeed the English troops should be praised." Like other senior Japanese officers, he condemned retreat and saluted standing to the end.

The Japanese trooping into Hong Kong the day after the British surrendered on Christmas Day, 1941. *University of Hong Kong History Archives*

"Jolo was successfully occupied this morning," he also recorded. Southwest of Mindanao, Jolo was a small undefended Philippine island east of Borneo, where the British were fighting off a second Japanese landing attempt on Sarawak. (Mili, to the far northeast, had been occupied easily on the fifteenth.) At Kuching, the capital of the semi-independent protectorate with a ruling "White Rajah," third in the family line, who had left Sarawak for Sydney, Australia, "enemy ships attacked one destroyer, *Sagiri,* besides four [troop] transports. Torpedoes struck the [destroyer], and she sank. . . . Half of the crew were saved." Soon after, a minesweeper and transport went down in the bay off Kuching. The Southern Expeditionary Force had asked for air support from carriers, but there was "no spare strength." Kuching was overwhelmed, more expensively than anticipated, beginning the movement south into Dutch-held Borneo.

What Ugaki did not note was that on December 25 the Japanese celebrated not the Western Christmas but the fifteenth anniversary of the succession of Emperor Hirohito to the Imperial Throne, according to tradition, the 124th direct descendant of Jimmu, legendary first ruler of the empire of the Rising Sun. All over the Home Islands, and wherever loyal Japanese lived abroad, festive toasts invoked the imperial reign.

From the emptying Marsman Building in Manila, bombed on Christmas Day, Admiral Hart, uninformed in advance by MacArthur about the open-city declaration and the withdrawal to Corregidor, telegraphed the general furiously, "While, as you have been repeatedly informed, it has been our intent to carry on the war here from submarines as long as possible—this denial of the use of the facilities within the metropolitan area very much shortens the period during which these operations can be carried out from here." Hart would have to evacuate, and leave behind for destruction, the remaining fuel storage facilities at Cavite. He ordered the disabling of the moored submarine tender *Canopus,* which could no longer cope with the open sea. In mid-February what was left of his command in the Indies would be put— briefly—under a Dutch admiral, after which Hart returned disconsolately to the United States (via Australia and Africa) to retire.

Another of many problem vessels in Philippine waters was the Guam station ship *Gold Star.* When Guam vanished into Japanese occupation, the freighter, en route home, had returned to Malangas on the southern coast of Mindanao and then to Cebu in the mid-Philippines. Its hold included coal, a thousand tons of cement, a thousand tons of rice, fifteen hundred cases of San Miguel beer, thirty cases of Scotch whiskey, Christmas toys for children of Guam personnel—now captives—and crates of bubble gum. New orders were to offload instead at Port Darwin in Australia, where the rigidly unionized longshoremen bridled about hauling any American cargo ashore, even the five thousand drums of cement, in which the inadequate and overstretched facilities were in short supply. After several days of delays, the Harbor Master "graciously allowed the *Gold Star* the use of an anti-submarine net crane, not needed in its primary function at night." In darkness the crew offloaded everything, including the cement, distributing provisions among American warships arriving at Darwin.

"YESTERDAY—a long day in the train," Oliver Harvey wrote. "When it got light to-day we were getting near Murmansk." Five hours later, at about noon, the returning British diplomats reached the dilapidated subarctic city and were driven sixteen miles to the anchorage for their ship and the treacherous voyage back to Scotland. "We did not sail until about 4:30 P.M. owing to some confusion over our luggage which was sent off to another ship by mistake. I thought we would never get off. It took about an hour to get down out of the estuary into the open sea, and then we were [in] for it! Very rough, ship pitching in all directions—no Xmas dinner for me! I rushed to my cabin, piled all my coats on, [and] went to bed practically in my clothes it was so bitter—far the coldest spot in all our journey." Harvey made no mention as to how Anthony Eden fared.

The train from precarious Moscow had bypassed even more precarious Leningrad, which had been cut off from land communication with the rest of Russia since September, but for a narrow, heavily forested, 220-mile route, often shelled, to Tikhvin to the west, recaptured only on December 9. Surfaced with logs and branches, the crude road sometimes lay above the many frozen workmen who had died of exposure or shellfire building it. The alternate "Road of Life" across broad Lake Ladoga to the north had not been available until November 26, when the surface had iced over to eight inches thickness, enough to bear the weight of supply trucks. On Christmas Day, when 3,700 inhabitants in Leningrad died of starvation or the bitter cold, the daily bread ration was increased from 8 to 10.5 ounces.

A crude method of making cellulose flour from shell packing had been developed at the Leningrad Scientific Institute, and wallpaper was stripped where possible to salvage the paste for what was called bread. Little fuel was available for cooking or heating; sanitation and medicines were rare. A city official in Leningrad, which would be blockaded for nine hundred days, wrote, "Death would overtake people in all kinds of circumstances. While they were on the streets they would fall down, never to rise again, or in their houses, where they would fall asleep and never awake; in factories where they would collapse while at work. There was no transport, and the dead body would usually be put on a hand-sleigh drawn by two or three members of the dead man's family; often, wholly exhausted during the long trek to the cemetery, they would abandon the body halfway, leaving the authorities to deal with it." At the Piskarevskoye Cemetery on the northern edge of the city, once and now again St. Petersburg, 800,000 dead during the siege would be buried.

<hr />

RARELY SEEN AT RELIGIOUS SERVICES at home, Churchill accompanied the President to the Foundry Methodist Church, "surrounded," Colonel Ian Jacob recorded in his diary, "by bevies of G-men, armed with Tommy-guns and revolvers." (The Secret Service had inspected the area in advance and returned, not quite inconspicuously.) Roosevelt seldom attended church in Washing-

Roosevelt and Churchill attending Foundry Methodist Church on Christmas morning, 1941. Mrs. Roosevelt is second from left. *Franklin D. Roosevelt Presidential Library*

ton because of the disruptions which security details created and the awkwardness of fitting his locked and then unlocked leg braces into a pew—and he did not want to be exposed in a wheelchair on an aisle. Asked why he wanted to forgo an Episcopal service on Christmas morning, he explained, "What's the matter? I like to sing hymns with the Methodys." And as the White House party set off in a queue of black automobiles past LaFayette and Farragut Squares for the church on 16th Street, its original building constructed in 1815 on land furnished by Henry Foxall, whose foundry had made weapons for George Washington's army to fight the British, Roosevelt quipped, "It is good for Winston to sing hymns with the Methodys."

Lilies on the altar, the *Washington Post* observed, were in memory of the President's mother, Sara. Roosevelt and Churchill sat in the fourth pew as the minister prayed for "those who are dying on land and sea this Christmas morning" and for his special guest from Britain who was leading "his valiant people even through blood and sweat and tears to a new world where men may dwell together, none daring to molest or make afraid." The congregation sang "O' Little Town of Bethlehem," which the PM had never heard before Christmas Eve. The lyrics were by an Episcopal priest, Phillips Brooks, rector of the Church of the Holy Trinity in Philadelphia, in 1868, with music by his organist, Lewis Redner. The lines had a special resonance in wartime:

> Yet in thy dark street shineth
> The everlasting light;
> The hopes and fears of all the years
> Are met in thee tonight.

Churchill—not a churchgoer at home—told Dr. Wilson that the service was "uplifting and restful."

Both Roosevelt and Churchill spent much of the afternoon reading and sending radiograms. Hong Kong had fallen, a not unexpected but costly embarrassment for Britain. Churchill had drawn a Canadian brigade for the indefensible colony, more to boost local morale than to bolster security. Two thousand Canadians were among the casualties—and the PM was planning a quick trip to Canada, where he would have some explaining to do. He reported to John Curtin, the Australian Prime Minister, that Roosevelt had agreed to divert weapons and troops earmarked for the Philippines to prop up Singapore if they could not be forced through to MacArthur and "to send substantial United States forces to Australia, where the Americans are anxious to establish important bases for the war against Japan."

American lines of communication to Australia, as a base of operations to defeat Japan, had become the only realistic priority on the Pacific Rim. Washington had no intentions of pouring troops down a Singapore sump and could not alter the finality of the Philippines. But when Roosevelt's alleged intentions, embroidered by Churchill, reached General Marshall—the military leaders on both sides were working through the holiday—he called in Hap Arnold and Ike Eisenhower and took them with him to Secretary Stimson's office to protest the apparent selling out of the Philippines, none of them realizing that MacArthur had just abandoned Manila, effectively relinquishing Luzon and soon the rest of the Philippines, to Japan. Without thinking through the reality that no American replenishment of Singapore nor of the Philippines would happen and that the President's radioed offer to MacArthur was largely rhetoric, Stimson telephoned the White House. Reaching Harry Hopkins, he declared that if the President was going to agree to "this kind of foolishness," he would have to get a new secretary of war.

Meeting with Stimson and the service chiefs at the White House, Roosevelt would downplay as a "misrepresentation" an alleged arrangement with Churchill to send American troops to Singapore. He had only ordered the redirection toward Singapore of an American ship carrying British troops to Ceylon. Hopkins assured the American chiefs that the White House would prevent further Churchillian misunderstandings, and Roosevelt offered on the record to build up a presence in Australia "toward operations to the north, including, of course, the Philippines."

Late on Christmas afternoon the chiefs of staff and their deputies convened in the refurbished World War I relic of the Old Munitions Building, a meeting that would break up at 5:20. Psychologically and strategically, whatever the losses anticipated on the Pacific Rim, Roosevelt had emphasized that he wanted "to have troops somewhere in active fighting across the Atlantic."

His priorities unchanged, he proposed a Germany-first war while holding what could be held in the Pacific. MacArthur would claim that the President was cajoled by Churchill into emphasizing Europe, but in a redraft of British proposals prepared on the voyage across, General Marshall and Admiral Stark had summed up the American position in two blunt paragraphs that reiterated pre–Pearl Harbor policy:

1. At the A-B [American-British] Staff Conversations in February 1941 [well before Pearl Harbor], it was agreed that Germany was the predominant member of the Axis Powers, and consequently the Atlantic and European area was considered to be the decisive theatre.

2. Much has happened since . . . , but notwithstanding the entry of Japan into the War, our view remains that Germany is still the prime enemy and her defeat is the key to victory. Once Germany is defeated, the collapse of Italy and the defeat of Japan must follow.

Secretary Stimson was well aware of that, but in misinterpreting the redirection of a single American troopship transporting no Americans, he wrote in his diary, "I think he [FDR] felt that he had pretty nearly burned his fingers and had called this subsequent meeting to make up for it. All things considered, this has been a strange and distressful Christmas."

Both allies were proposing strategies to relieve pressure upon Russia by forcing the *Wehrmacht* to withdraw some divisions to the West. Churchill pressed his military chiefs to consider another landing in Norway, where he had already failed, at Narvik, in 1940. To the alarm of the British, Roosevelt had suggested to Churchill a costly feint toward occupied France, which at the least would get Hitler's attention. Something had to be done. It was crucial to keep Stalin from pursuing a separate peace, which could divert millions of the enemy toward the West. Easier pickings, with the same outcome, the British continued to suggest, would be Vichy French Africa.

Discovering from talks with Marshall, King, and their deputies that Roosevelt only conferred with his service chiefs as he felt necessary rather than on a regular schedule, John Dill cabled Sir Alan Brooke, chief of the Imperial General Staff, with concern that American military cohesion "belongs to the days of George Washington." On the civilian side of running the war, FDR's managerial style was to employ a plethora of people squabbling over their overlapping responsibilities. It was not so with the military dimension. General Marshall was fully in charge. FDR respected his judgment and largely left him to run the war. He may have overruled Marshall only once or twice during the entire course of planning. Churchill, however, as Dill well knew, constantly interfered in strategic matters, exasperating the PM's military chiefs, yet he contended that he was entitled to do so as self-appointed Minister of Defence.

<hr />

ROOSEVELT'S DRAFT of a declaration by the "Associated Powers" linked with the United States and Britain, first drawn up by Cordell Hull, and now conflated into a joint statement by Churchill, had been radioed to London on Christmas Eve. By the next afternoon the White House had received a cable from Clement Attlee on behalf of the War Cabinet, conveying its surprise at the sweeping concept and hoping that all allies willing to sign it should be given that opportunity. The advice from London was that such participation would furnish proof "that this war is being waged for the freedom of the small nations as well as the great powers."

Despite that achievement, in which Secretary Hull could take pride, another and smaller ongoing event rankled him. While he was struggling to maintain ties with wretched Vichy, a formal Christmas Day plebiscite had been arranged by Admiral Émile Muselier for the seized islets of Saint-Pierre and Miquelon, specks under the French flag twelve miles south of Newfoundland. Despite contrary assurances of their integrity by Charles de Gaulle's London-based Free French, a small force of three corvettes and a submarine the day before, without firing a shot, had upset the status quo. Its few hundred male citizens (females were excluded) voted 98 percent in favor of adhering to Free France. However arbitrary the occupation and its confirmation of the ambitions of de Gaulle, whose relationship with Roosevelt would never be better than sour, territory and people had been liberated for the first time in the war. It seemed an unexpected holiday gift.

Only a one-star general, de Gaulle had assumed for himself the mantle of the leaderless French resistance and was demonstrating that he would not be a pawn. Tall and imposing, he was still little known in France, but Vichy, nevertheless, anxious about his growing mystique, portrayed him in press caricatures as short and fat. Pleased with the small but symbolic coup, the *New York Post* wrote of "great joy this Christmas Day." Invoking French literature, the *New York Times* editorialized about "a [military] display of style and manners in the best tradition of Alexander Dumas." The *Christian Science Monitor*, praising "an initiative and flair that have often been lacking in Allied strategy," titled its commentary "*Beau Geste.*"

A week earlier an aide to Rear Admiral Chester W. Nimitz, head of the Bureau of Navigation at the Navy Department Building on Constitution Avenue, had picked up the office phone and heard the caller ask, "May I speak to Chester?" It seemed undignified to Lieutenant Howell Lamar until the voice added, "This is the President. Put him on the phone." Two hours later Nimitz returned from the White House with orders to command what was left of the Pacific Fleet, and on December 19 left with Lamar, both in civilian clothes and under assumed names, by rail from Union Station to the West Coast. (Nimitz was advised not to chance flying across the country in winter weather.) Rear Admiral Husband E. Kimmel, tarnished by unreadiness at Pearl Harbor, had been sacked. He was ordered to remain in Hawaii, as was Lieutenant General Walter C. Short, also replaced, for Justice Roberts's hearings.

At seven on the grey Christmas morning Nimitz's Coronado (PB2Y) flying boat landed in the east loch of the harbor. Nimitz was still in civilian garb. The whaleboat taking the party to shore was splashed with black oil seeping from sunken ships; everyone stood awkwardly. "What news of the relief of Wake?" Nimitz asked, and learned that reinforcements had been recalled as hopeless and that the atoll had been surrendered. Remaining silent, he grimly watched the floating debris and oil slicks, and the bloated corpses still surfacing from submerged wrecks.

⚬⚬⚬

WITH THE WEATHER NOT COLD ENOUGH for a white Christmas, a light drizzle was now falling in the Capital environs. Soon after six the Marshalls, who did little formal dining at Fort Myer, entertained some of the ranking British contingent not invited to the White House: Ambassador and Lady Halifax, Lord Beaverbrook, Admiral Pound, Air Marshal Portal, and Field Marshal Dill. When Katherine Marshall discovered belatedly, as guests were gathering, that December 25 was also Sir John Dill's sixtieth birthday, she sent Sergeant James Powder, her husband's paragon of efficiency, to find a cake and candles. Despite Christmas closings, he returned with both and also with miniature British and American flags as decoration. As they were popped into the icing, Dill confided that he had not had his birthday celebrated since he was a small boy. Removing some of the flags afterward to insert a knife into the cake, he discovered that they were stamped "Made in Japan." When a Western Union messenger arrived to perform a singing "Happy Birthday to You" telegram—Powder had thought of everything—he was intercepted by a Secret Service detail. There was wartime security somewhere.

At eight Churchill dined with the Roosevelts at the White House. A turkey dinner for sixty using gold-plated flatware from the Grover Cleveland administration a half-century earlier hardly resembled a business meeting, although several presidential associates were seated as well as the Morgenthaus and Olav and Marthe of Norway. FDR had invited some cousins and some friends, among them financier Bernard Baruch and a former Under Secretary of the Navy Garrison Norton. Champagne was liberally served after each of many toasts, the President recalling in his toast to Britain that King George VI and Queen Elizabeth had dined in the same room in 1939, a beginning of the "coming together" of the nations, which, he vowed, would continue after victory.

Churchill asked for Johnnie Walker in his glass and seemed silent and preoccupied. Bad news kept coming—and despite all of it he had to deliver a stirring address the next day to an unpredictable audience. Garrison Norton recalled that after dinner, newsreels and the film adaptation of Dickens' *Oliver Twist* were shown. As the reel was being changed, Churchill rose and explained, "I must prepare for tomorrow." He was working on his speech to Congress and would continue long into the night and again in the morning.

The PM had begun drafting it as cocktail time approached—the President referred to the sacred interlude as "Children's

Hour." Mixing and serving drinks from a seated position was one of the few physical activities he could accomplish with an audience. As a White House assistant put it, FDR "was trapped in that chair and could not go out and mix and mingle." The "Children's Hour" and his press conferences, where he could banter with reporters from his desk, were his opportunities to break out of the reality of confinement.

"At cocktail time," Mary Churchill recalled from her father's experience, "everything was beautifully stage-managed so that [the President] could be in control, despite his disability. He would be wheeled in and then spun around to be at the drinks table, where he could reach everything. There were the bottles, there was the shaker, there was the ice. It was all beautifully done. There was never an effort or scurry. He loved the ceremony of making the drinks; it was rather like, 'Look, I can do it.' It was formidable. And you know you were supposed to hand him your glass, and not reach for anything else. It was a lovely performance."

Churchill was considering quoting in his address the next day a passage from the 112th Psalm. He knew the Bible as literature rather than from a pew. He wondered whether Roosevelt would approve of the choice. Dr. Wilson, accompanying Churchill, carried a copy to the libations, perhaps the first time that had been done in the years of the FDR presidency. "The PM took the Bible from me," Wilson noted in his diary, "and read his quotation to the President, who liked it." The verse was "He shall not be afraid of evil tidings; his heart is fixed, trusting in the Lord." It fit the circumstances.

December 26, 1941

I N T H E P H I L I P P I N E S the armies of General Homma were moving relentlessly toward Manila, where the anxious population awaited the inevitable. As telephone communication with Corregidor still existed, MacArthur called Carlos Romulo to unseal the proclamation declaring Manila an open city. Then Romulo was to slip across the bay to join the staff. Separately, MacArthur sent Sid Huff back to Manila to search in the general's bedroom for his prized old campaign hat and the Colt .45 he had carried in France in the last war. (He would wear both on his only brief trip across the bay to Bataan, which he made on January 10, stolidly leaning on his cane. A wax museum on Coney Island, eight thousand miles eastward, would soon feature a display, "MacArthur at Bataan.") "I think if you look in the dining room," MacArthur added, "you may see a bottle of Scotch. Just as well to bring that, too. It may be a long hard winter over here." Huff left in one of the fast PT (torpedo) boats remaining at the Rock.

Hoping to prevent the Japanese from seizing Jorge Vargas, Manuel Quezon tried using international law as it applied to local officials, telling his executive secretary by telephone, "Jorge, you are appointed Mayor of the City of Greater Manila." But Vargas not only had no paper evidence; the Japanese seldom respected international law. Yet because they wanted what would be

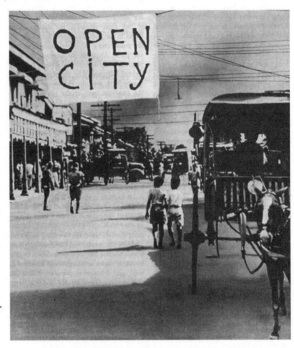

"Open City" placard hoisted by Manila residents the day after Christmas, 1941. *United States Army Center of Military History*

the slim authority of a national official, he was recognized as mayor and requisitions would be issued in his name without notifying him.

The withdrawals of American and Filipino forces into Bataan would be a litany of hardship. The puny Philippine excuses for divisions had little to fight with. American regiments were undermanned and underarmed. Captain Russell W. Volckmann of the 11th Infantry was ordered to leave behind the equipment his troops could not carry through open country. No roads existed to move his trucks and other vehicles. His men had to conduct a defensive retreat with no food, supplies, equipment, or ammunition other than what they could carry on their backs. Volkmann found that thirty miles of the route followed railway trackage, and he located on sidings eleven freight cars and a nearby engine. Fortunately his regiment, like the others, lacked numbers. He jammed his men into the freight cars until there was little breathing space, then ordered truck drivers to follow gingerly, bumping along the crossties.

Another understrength regiment, the 26th Cavalry, ordered to withdraw and to destroy seven bridges as they did, lost one-third of its personnel and animals killed, wounded, and missing in accomplishing the mission. Three hundred Philippine Scouts from Fort McKinley in Manila were ordered south, rather than to Bataan, to help the frail 1st Philippine Division hold back the Japanese moving toward the city from Lamon Bay. The Scouts hailed taxicabs to drive them to the rapidly receding front but could do nothing useful and retreated on foot. In Manila itself, walking wounded at military hospitals were taken by water to Bataan; 350 more critically injured at the army's Sternberg Hospital were abandoned. Nihro Katsumi, the Japanese Consul General in Manila, still in deliberately loose custody, made arrangements by radio for safe passage of the *Mactan,* a Philippines interisland ship, to evacuate to Australia the unwanted casualties, accompanied by one American doctor, one American nurse, and several Filipino doctors and nurses.

Rank had its dubious privileges. Evicting the Corregidor staff, MacArthur's entourage moved into Topside, the clutch of houses at a six hundred–foot elevation near a concrete barracks. The arrangement lasted until showers of air raids forced them into quarters in the Rock's mile-long Malinta Tunnel, the headquarters of last resort.

As the venerable four-stacker destroyer *Pillsbury* left Manila Bay for the Indies, a flashing light signal came from Corregidor, "Proceed on mission assigned. Good luck and God's speed." Passengers taken on included, J. Daniel Mullin noted in his diary, "Admiral Hart's excellent Purple Code Gang." The navy in September 1940 had broken the Japanese diplomatic cipher, code-named "Purple," but—unfortunately—had not been able to read the parallel Admiralty code in time to prevent Pearl Harbor. Taking on passengers by launch was the four-stacker *Peary*, also headed for Balikpapan. *Peary* had been hastily patched together after the Cavite raids, having lost twenty-three crew dead and missing, a foremast severed, and its antennas and rangefinder destroyed. *Pillsbury* had lost twelve dead and missing, a guywire to the mainmast severed, a torpedo tube mount destroyed, and a fuel tank punctured below the waterline. Two days later, with its damaged tank sealed, it moored in Borneo and at a half hour before midnight took on 103,807 gallons of fuel.

When the launch from the Rock pulled away, *Peary* took aboard its nine evacuees. Lieutenant John M. Bermingham, its captain, advised Ensign Philip Joyce, "In event of action at the Bay's entrance, have them assemble in the forward crew's quarters. Get a complete list of names, file or service numbers for the log." Bermingham had been deputy to Lieutenant Commander Harry H. Keith, *Peary*'s former captain, who had been wounded

Destroyer *USS Peary. Naval Historical Center*

in both knees at Cavite and hospitalized. Already thirty-six and a 1929 Annapolis grad, Bermingham had waited a long time in the slow-to-promote peacetime navy for a command.

Seaman Lester Harris, the navigator, an old China hand who had seen Japanese mistreatment of women, looking up from the inland charts he had ironed out after their immersion in Manila Bay at Cavite, remarked, "I thought that the boat would bring some of the nurses out. It's a shame to leave them." MacArthur kept them at Corregidor, where, after months of bombardment, they would become prisoners of war on May 7, 1942. (The general, his family, and his personal staff had been evacuated south on four PT-boats on March 11.)

Brought aboard *Peary*, its white surface frills of peacetime now being repainted in camouflage green to be less visible from the air, were "cryptographic aids" (apparently codebooks), a "Purple" coding machine, and a radio receiver—"all welcome equipment." Seamen were especially grateful to be able to pick up the BBC, as it was, they had learned, "the most reliable and truthful," however disheartening. As the destroyer began moving out, the C.O. directed a signalman to flash, "Passengers and cargo aboard. Request permission to proceed on mission assigned." One guest was Rear Admiral F. W. Rockwell, Hart's deputy, who had dodged Japanese bombs at Cavite, losing everything but the sweaty clothes on his back. He "half smiled" at the signal, "for the ship could be seen as already underway." Permission was granted, with a "Good luck and safe harbor."

<hr />

IN MALAYA, on small boats and rafts, the Japanese began crossing the broad Perak at nightfall. Moving tanks and heavy vehicles across the river would require sturdy bridges. The blown spans had to be repaired or replaced. Infantry awaiting orders to take Ipoh and Kuala Lumpur were as reluctant to move as their officers were impatient. On their way through rubber plantations as they advanced, Japanese troops had caught monkeys in the trees by offering them fruit and were amusing themselves by watching them. Others had bathed in emptied oil drums. Soon soldiers from the 5th Division and the Imperial Guards Division were across the Perak, British headquarters reporting three full divisions massing against them. Only a third of the Imperial Guards had arrived in Malaya, one regiment of the 5th was still in Shanghai, and most of the 18th Division was still awaiting shipment. Effectively, Lieutenant General Tomoyuki Yamashita had only eight regiments pushing down the main trunk road and the western coast road toward Malacca. The underwhelmed British forces backing into Singapore continued to be reinforced by troopships docking into irrelevance, and worse.

"Boxing Day" to the British, the traditional post-Christmas holiday, meant nothing in occupied and ravaged Hong Kong; yet in doomed Singapore colonists and troops celebrated with toasts empty of meaning but stimulated by wine or whiskey certain otherwise to fall to the enemy. Across the time zones in isolated Malta, surviving despite daily air raids and a Mediterranean swarming with Axis submarines, J. Q. Hughes wrote indelicately about his sloshed superiors, "Sgt. Major Hunt and Sgt. Sandy were quite incapable and more often than not unconscious for two days." They had begun drinking on Christmas Day. "One officer attended a Court Martial in which all the members were drunk, and the proceedings were thus postponed for several days."

The *Ford*'s log in Surabaja reported on the day after Christmas, "Minor repair work being accomplished on *Pope* and *Ford* by tender personnel. Liberty for both ships. Ensign Cross had some errands to carry out. . . . On his way he passed several shops near the Hotel Oranje. He saw a very beautiful mixed Dutch and

Indonesian girl. This was too much. After passing several times, he worked up courage and introduced himself. Her name was Wente, and like many, spoke passable English. She was agreeable to having dinner with Cross and his roommate for whom she would find a friend, a couple of days hence." For the moment it was a good war.

AT *Wolfsschanze*—Wolf's Lair—Hitler's concealed but lavish headquarters bunkers near Rastenburg in East Prussia, Field Marshal Gunther von Kluge announced the dismissal from his tank command of armor expert General Heinz Guderian, whose *Blitzkreig* had quickly beaten France the year before. Retreating to save his 2nd Panzer Army, Guderian had defied orders to halt in place. Summoned to the Führer on December 20, he endured five hours of admonishment for timidity and for having "too much pity" for his troops. The ground was frozen to a depth of five feet, Guderian explained. Hitler knew it. He had already confessed publicly that there was such a shortage of winter uniforms that Goebbels had mounted a massive "Winter Aid" appeal, urging Germans to send warm clothing and shoes of any sort, especially ski wear, to collection points for the East. On national radio Goebbels had declared, less gently than had Hitler, that "people at home would not deserve a moment's peace if a single German soldier was exposed to the harshness of winter without articles of warm clothing." Film, theater and sports figures were sent about the country to promote the effort, inadvertently publicizing the failure to win the Russian war, as once predicted, before winter.

The hurried campaign, due to have ended symbolically at Christmas, would be extended to January 11, amassing 67 million

The Russian bear emerging from a Christmas tree decoration. *Cartoon from Portsmouth, NH,* Herald, *December 26, 1941*

articles, much of the collection unusable or beyond any means of transporting and distributing it to the front. Hitler had ignored the implications of the "Winter Aid" promotion in berating Guderian. "Do you think Frederick the Great's grenadiers were anxious to die?" he charged. "They wanted to live, too, but the king was right in asking them to sacrifice themselves. I believe that I, too, am entitled to ask any German soldier to lay down his life." Later Hitler desperately needed Guderian and restored him to duty.

<hr />

GENERAL SIR ALAN BROOKE, Dill's successor, convened a chiefs of staff meeting in London on Boxing Day morning, discussing "reinforcing of Far East and Fiji Islands etc.," he noted in his diary, inexplicably pairing the two as if of equal consequence. "In afternoon rung up by Attlee," he added, "to find out whether we were ready for a Defence Committee meeting to keep Australians quiet as they were fretting about [providing] reinforcements to Singapore." Australians in Singapore destined for Japanese POW camps had their parallel in Canadians already captive in Hong Kong—imported to defend the indefensible.

Waiting until the day after Christmas, to drain less joy out of the holiday, Leon Henderson, Price Administrator and manager of wartime rationing, announced in Washington that as of January 3, ordinary motorists, including taxi drivers and traveling salesmen, would be prohibited from buying new tires without certificates validating need for essential services involving health, safety, and industrial operations. He made no reference to the ongoing Japanese seizure of rubber plantations in Southeast Asia or the sluggish and reluctant domestic production of synthetic rubber. Because milk and associated products were often trucked home-to-home along city streets, Henderson suggested pooling vehicles and routes for delivery services. Certificates would soon be needed even for purchasing retreaded and recapped tires. Shops would run short of rubber gloves, overshoes, floor mats, garden hoses, and even hot-water bottles—but not under-the-counter condoms.

Although it was the day after Christmas, most members of Congress had remained in Washington as Churchill was to address a joint session of the Senate and House. He had given much thought to what he should say and called in one of his secretaries, Patrick Kinna, to take dictation while the PM was still in his morning bath—as not a minute could be wasted. He kept submerging his bulk in the steaming suds, and when he "surfaced," he would dictate a few more words or sentences. Soon, Kinna recalled, "he got out of the bath when his devoted valet, [Frank] Sawyers, draped an enormous bath-towel around him. He walked into his adjoining bedroom followed by me, notebook in hand, and continued to dictate while pacing up and down."

Eventually the towel fell to the floor. Unconcerned, the PM continued pacing the room, dictating all the time.

Suddenly, Kinna recalled, "President Roosevelt [in his wheelchair] entered the bedroom and saw the British Prime Minister completely naked walking around the room dictating to me. WSC never being lost for words said, 'You see, Mr President, I have nothing to conceal from you.'"

Harry Hopkins, across the hall, learned of the incident and the President's abortive attempt to apologize for the intrusion. He enjoyed retelling the story, which was assigned a variety of wrong dates. Hopkins's friend Robert Sherwood, a Roosevelt speech writer, later asked Churchill about it. "I could not possibly have made such a statement like that," Churchill insisted. "The President himself would have been aware that it was not strictly true." To Churchill the episode had reduced his dignity.*

From morning into night, the PM would carry a tot of brandy about, often refilling his glass. Late one evening when Hopkins and Churchill went to the map room for a briefing, the conversation got around to the PM's liquid capacity. Hopkins picked up a pencil and calculated on the basis of the daily intake he observed how many tank cars of brandy Churchill had consumed in his lifetime. He offered a number. "Tank cars or tankards," dismissed Churchill. "I thought I had done rather better than that."

ROOSEVELT WOULD NOT ACCOMPANY the Prime Minister along Pennsylvania Avenue to the Capitol. Churchill was to have

---

*In his memoirs Churchill, ignoring Kinna's recollection, would own up to it but dated it as the morning of January 1, 1942, which is less logical and far less likely.

the occasion for himself. FDR wished "the Prime" luck and planned to listen on the radio. "There seemed to be great crowds along the broad approaches," Churchill wrote in his memoirs, "but the security precautions, which in the United States go far beyond British custom, kept them a long way off, and two or three motorcars filled with armed plainclothes policemen clustered around as escort. On getting out I wished to walk up to the cheering masses in a strong mood of brotherhood, but this was not allowed."

As soon as the PM was seen being accompanied down the aisle in the House chamber toward the rostrum, a friendly roar could be heard on radios nationwide. "Congress Thrilled," a *New York Times* subheading reported. "Prime Minister Warns of Dark Days but Holds Victory Is Certain." He spoke through "a grille of microphones," capturing his audiences from the start. "I had never addressed a foreign Parliament before," Churchill recalled. "Yet to me, who could trace unbroken male descent on my mother's side through five generations from a lieutenant who served in George Washington's army, it was possible to feel a blood-right to address representatives of the great Republic in our common cause."

He was "greatly honored" at the invitation, he began:

The fact that my American forbears have for so many generations played their part in the life of the United States, and that here I am, as an Englishman, welcomed in your midst, makes this experience one of the most moving and thrilling in my life, which is already long and has not been entirely uneventful. I wish indeed that my mother, whose memory I cherish across the vale of years, could be here to see me. By the way, I can't help reflecting that if my father had been American and my mother British, instead of the other way round, I might have got here on my own. In that case this would not have been the first time you would have heard my voice. In that case I should not have needed any invitation, but if I had, it is hardly likely it would have been unanimous. So perhaps things are better as they are.

The informality and wit of his opening captured his audience, and the ringing cheers made it difficult to go on. He claimed to have found, in his few days in Washington, "an Olympian fortitude" and a sense of "inflexible purpose" as well as "confidence in the final outcome. We in Britain had the same feeling in our darkest days." He did not want to project an easy optimism. "Some people may be startled or momentarily depressed when, like your President, I speak of a long and hard war. But our peoples would rather know the truth, sombre though it might be." Whether "deliverance would come in 1942, 1943, or 1944" was up to "the grand proportions of human history."

Churchill elicited another roar when he asked, about the Japanese, obviously on the minds of most listeners, "What kind of a people do they think we are? Is it possible they do not realize that we shall never cease to persevere against them until they have been taught a lesson which they and the world will never forget?" He wondered why, as their "intricate preparations" for war had gone on so long, "they did not choose our [worst] moment of weakness eighteen months ago. Viewed quite dispassionately, in spite of the losses we have suffered and the further punishment we will have to take, it certainly appears to be an irrational act. . . . They must now know that the stakes for which they have decided to play are mortal."

In a house full of stubborn isolationists now reluctant warriors, he did not hesitate to blame passivity in his host's country as well as his own, particularly for the European war, because

Five or six years ago it would have been easy, without shedding a drop of blood, for the United States and Great Britain to have insisted on fulfilment of the disarmament clauses of the treaties which Germany signed after the Great War; that also would have been the opportunity for assuring to Germany those raw materials which we declared in the Atlantic Charter should not be denied to any nation, victor or vanquished. That chance has passed. It is gone. Prodigious hammer-strokes have been needed to bring us together again.

Because it was the season of Christmas, he concluded with an upbeat peroration calculated to appeal to the churched. Only a "blind soul," he concluded, could not see "that some great purpose and design is being worked out here below, of which we have the honour to be the faithful servants. It is not given to us to peer into the mysteries of the future. Still, I avow my hope and faith, sure and inviolate, that in the days to come the British and American peoples will for their own safety and for the good of all wall together side by side in majesty, in justice, and in peace."

As Churchill was escorted off the podium he raised his hand and flashed, with two fingers, his familiar "V for Victory" gesture. Frenzied cheers followed, and others in the chamber, including Chief Justice Harlan Fiske Stone, returned the salute. "You could follow that fellow anywhere," enthused Senator Millard Tydings of Maryland. "It was a clever speech, and one that generally will appeal to the American people," isolationist senator Burton K. Wheeler of Montana conceded. At lunch afterward with senior legislators whom he had not selected, he met Wheeler and told him that the speech downplayed criticism of prewar attitudes, for "if the present criticizes the past, there is not much hope for the future." It was a conciliatory remark but contradicted by Churchill's willingness to blame Western passivity. Leaving, he waved to crowds still waiting outside to see him. "Then the Secret Service men and their cars closed round and took me back to the White House, where the President, who had listened in, told me I had done quite well."

Listening on the radio in Norris, Tennessee, from which he directed the Tennessee Valley Authority, the massive power and flood-control system that was a New Deal initiative, David Lilienthal judged the speech a "masterpiece" with "wonderful balance and alliteration." At one point, he marveled, Churchill "made a growling sound . . . like the British lion!" At Passfield Corner, the home in Liphook, Hampshire, of old Socialists Beatrice and Sidney Webb, now in their feeble eighties, the couple listened, at 7:30 P.M. British time, "with an all-out admiration," Beatrice wrote in her diary, to the "oration" to Congress of their old Tory political enemy, Winston Churchill, and reveled loyally in the "deafening" applause. "His opening allusion to his American mother was perfect in its tact; the summary of past events, of present difficulties, of future prospects . . . was all exactly suited to the occasion." As one who saw Stalin's Russia as without flaw, Mrs. Webb perceived, nevertheless, its "one weak point." It was Churchill's "tacit refusal to recognize the Soviet Union as the equal to the U.K. and the U.S.A. in determining the terms of the eventual peace and practically the paramount power in deciding what shall be the new international order. . . ."

Mackenzie King arrived in Washington too late for Churchill's performance, his special train from Ottawa arriving at Union Station at 3:45 P.M. FDR's aide General "Pa" Watson met him and escorted him to the Mayflower Hotel, where he checked in before his appointment with Secretary Hull at the State Department, after which he was to see Roosevelt and Churchill, who were busy with larger matters than the islets off Newfoundland which were roiling relations with the Vichy French.

Although Churchill had already suggested feints against the coastline of occupied Europe to divert German troops from the Eastern front and spread thinner those guarding what Hitler referred to as the Atlantic Wall, he was closemouthed about one already in progress that dawn. "Operation Archery" had targeted

Vågsøy Island, at the mouth of Nordfjord, far above Bergen. A force of 570 Commandos supported by the cruiser *Kenya* and four destroyers (in short supply elsewhere), and RAF bombers and fighters, went ashore to raid fish-oil production plants and to induce the Germans to transfer more strength to the far north of Norway. One of the Commando officers was Major "Mad Jack" Churchill. Thirty-five and no relation to the Prime Minister, "Mad Jack" was born in Hong Kong and was a between-the-wars soldier reactivated in 1939. An eccentric who coveted danger, he carried a longbow and bagpipes into action, and with a Manchester regiment in France in 1940 he brought down a German sergeant with his bow and arrows, very likely the only such fatality in the war. Emerging from his landing craft at Nordfjord, he began playing "The March of the Cameron Men" on his bagpipes and heaved a grenade.

Like most Commando operations it was a very mixed success. When the British, with a dozen Norwegians from an exile company, began their withdrawal at 2:00 P.M.—the day darkened early in the north—they evacuated to their landing craft under greater fire than anticipated. Unknown to the strike force, a *Gebirgsjäger* (mountain troop) unit was on leave there from the Russian front, and house-to-house fighting broke out in the town of Måløy. Commandos claimed 120 enemy dead and took 98 prisoners. Their chief prize was a German naval codebook. The Royal Navy lost four killed, and the Commandos seventeen. The commander of the Norwegian unit died in an attack on German headquarters. The RAF lost eight planes.

Hitler sent thirty thousand more troops to safeguard Norway. Jack Churchill received the Military Cross. Later he would lead Commando units in Sicily and at Salerno, after which he received the DSO. Still carrying his bagpipes, he led Commandos supporting Marshal Tito in Yugoslavia, where he was taken prisoner and brought to Berlin for interrogation, then incarcerated at

"Operation Archery" on the Norwegian coast concludes with the evacuation of British commandos, December 27, 1941. *Imperial War Museum*

notorious Sachenhausen, from which he and an RAF officer escaped and were recaptured. In April 1945 Churchill was sent to a prison camp in the Tyrol which the Germans then abandoned. He walked 150 miles to Verona, where he met an American tank column. Eager for more, he rejoined the British and was sent to Burma, arriving too late for action. "If it wasn't for those damn Yanks," he complained, "we could have kept this war going for another ten years!" Yet he found more war, playing an archer in a film version of *Ivanhoe* in 1946, then qualifying as a parachutist and joining the Highland Light Infantry in Palestine. There, as the British Mandate ended meanly in 1948, he came to the aid, with twelve of his men, of the Hadassah Hospital convoy evacuating patients and medical staff from Mount Scopus under withering fire from the Arabs. In Australia afterward he was an instructor at the land-air warfare school. Retiring in 1959, he returned to England, where he died in Surrey at ninety. Winston Churchill must have felt some pride in his feisty namesake.

AT 4:30 THAT AFTERNOON, Roosevelt and Churchill and their military and civilian advisers met in the White House. It was, Secretary Stimson noted in his diary, "a sort of interim conference to see how the Chiefs of Staff had been getting on in their conferences and everything seems to be going well." Field Marshal Dill reviewed once more the chancy "proposition" of sending troops to Vichy French North Africa, and General Marshall, replying to FDR's question as to whether that would "impair" supplying England, said that it would depend on how large an invasion force "was necessary to appeal to the French in such a way that the occupation would be expedited." Employing his usual salty language, Admiral King seized upon the "impairment," as Marshall cloaked it in his minutes, contending that a North African operation, soaking up shipping in short supply, would delay his convoying American troops and war materiel to Britain, which was far more crucial than a dicey adventure to Morocco or Algeria.

With both sides embarrassed by King's choice of metaphors, Churchill intervened to emphasize the need to relieve British troops in Iceland and Northern Ireland for duty elsewhere and wondered what might be done to rescue the dire situation in Malaya and Singapore. Unity of command across Southeast Asia then came up, with Churchill observing that only where there was "a continuous line of battle," as in France in 1918, was such unity practical, and the operating areas this time were vast and widely separated, but Secretary Knox contended that a "scattered condition of command" was in itself an argument for unity, exercised somewhere, perhaps even from Washington.

While the conference continued, Secretary Hull sought compromises with Canadian Prime Minister Mackenzie King to cope with the embarrassing minor victory that had emerged the day before Christmas. Saint-Pierre and Miquelon had maintained a powerful radio station broadcasting Vichy propaganda to French-speaking Canadians and communicating with Vichy itself. The British also suspected that it was communicating cryptic data to German subs about convoys in the North Atlantic. To try to edge Vichy away, even slightly, from its Nazi overseers, the Americans and the British, including the Canadians, had not wanted to upset the status quo. De Gaulle called the seizure a purely internal French affair.

Cordell Hull, seventy and ailing, was furious at the caper, but the issue had not seemed of sufficient military importance to make the conference agenda. He determined to put it on his own agenda. For Hull it was a violation of the long-standing Monroe Doctrine of noninterference by outsiders in hemisphere territories. That post-Christmas afternoon he proposed to King unsuccessfully that the Gaullists be pressured to withdraw but that the operation of the islands' radio be placed under allied supervision.

In his diary Mackenzie King wrote, "I told him it would not do to have the Governor restored, as he was pro-Axis, and his wife a German. . . . Canadian feeling was relieved and pleased with the de Gaulle accomplishment. . . . We would have to be careful to see that whatever was done would not appear that we were sacrificing the Free French. I said to Mr. Hull I would try to get Mr. Churchill to view the matter in this way. Mr. Hull and I then went over to the White House where we joined the President and Mr. Churchill in the Oval Room at tea. . . ."

A 5:00 P.M., an armed Bureau of Printing and Engraving truck—from the agency that printed American currency—pulled up to a loading platform at the Library of Congress. Alongside was another vehicle with guards holding automatic weapons. Workmen loaded the sealed founding documents so carefully packed before Christmas and headed for Union Station. There the cargo was loaded into Compartment B, Car A-1, on the Pullman sleeper *Eastlake* of the Baltimore & Ohio Railroad. Secret Service agents moved into compartments on either side, and others manned the corridor. The train left the station at 6:30, en route to Louisville, Kentucky.

AT "TEA" IN THE WHITE HOUSE—King had sworn off alcohol for the duration—the French islets issue was largely settled. Mackenzie King mollified Hull by contending that the Secretary "had a better idea" than bringing the Governor back—"which was to let de Gaulle feel that, while he had been precipitate, he had cleared up a certain situation thereby making it possible to have the whole supervision of radio messages properly arranged for. . . . Mr. Hull said he thought he and I were 98 per cent agreed on what should be done. Mr. Roosevelt said he thought it would be best for Mr. Hull and me to work out a suggested arrangement and then it could be considered tomorrow." Churchill, armed with a scotch and soda, agreed. De Gaulle would be emboldened for further capers.

Before dinner that evening, which included White House friends, Churchill, Roosevelt and Hopkins, with Mackenzie King and Lord Beaverbrook, discussed further the problem of Far East command and its huge boundaries. Marshall defined the area as ABDA (American, British, Dutch, Australian). Churchill favored direction by a combined group in Washington. Roosevelt also wanted an on-site commander, intending, as Marshall had suggested to him, to propose Field Marshal Sir Archibald Wavell, then commanding British Far East forces from India. He had been successful against the Italians in Egypt and Libya, but nowhere else, and had the misfortune of commanding largely when his forces were disadvantaged. He had fought in the Boer War, lost an eye in the trenches in France in 1915, and became a proponent of tank warfare. Wavell was fluent in Russian, read Latin and Greek, and even wrote poetry. Other than his having commanded, without distinction, an operational theater (in the Middle East), nothing but his rank and availability made him a logical choice.

Churchill kept his dark suspicions to himself. Obviously, Wavell would be filling a slot until the reason for his command evaporated. Hopkins had already whispered to the PM, "Don't be in a hurry to turn down the proposal the President is going to make to you before you know who the man is we have in mind." Churchill's military deputy Colonel Ian Jacob, who must have intimated his concerns, noted in his diary that unity over such distances would be purely symbolic—that their new partners in arms "foresaw inevitable disasters in the Far East, and feared the force of the American public opinion which might so easily cast the blame . . . on to the shoulders of a British general."

After dinner, for a change of atmosphere, the President had a movie shown, *The Maltese Falcon,* with Humphrey Bogart as Sam Spade. Churchill stayed to the end, in the front row, commenting afterward about a parallel case he had encountered in the 1920s when he was home secretary. Then he retired to draft another major speech for a very different audience.

Mackenzie King had invited the PM to address the Canadian Parliament before the new year recess. Retiring to his rooms to work on the speech, Churchill attempted to open a window. "It was very stiff," he told Dr. Wilson the next morning. "I had to use considerable force and I noticed all at once that I was short of breath. I had a dull pain over my heart. It went down my left arm. It didn't last very long, but it has never happened before. What is it? Is my heart all right?"

The discomfort abated. He set to work into the night, then went to bed without alarming Wilson.

December 27, 1941

THE ASSOCIATED PRESS reported from a late afternoon MacArthur communiqué that heavy tank battles "raged inconclusively" south of Manila following the Lamon Bay landings. There was no mention that Manila had been abandoned. The tanks were a fiction. An unidentified army "spokesman" for the general advised falsely by radio that the fighting on Luzon was "going well." Francis Sayre, the American high commissioner for the Philippines, allegedly declared, "We will fight to the last man." (Sayre was already on Corregidor with his family and staff.)

Traversing the Sulu Sea, the inland Philippines passage already known as "the gauntlet," the destroyer *Peary* received a radio message that the Japanese were landing at Taytay, the northernmost harbor on long, narrow Palawan, the westernmost Philippine island. *Peary* altered course to the southeast, passing Panay and reaching Negros at 10:30 A.M. As she anchored, a flight of five twin-engine enemy bombers passed overhead, not seeing the four-stacker, whose crew was still spreading pungent green paint with mops. Torpedoman John Fero wisecracked, "Hell, if the Japs can't see us, they sure will be able to smell us." The next afternoon off the western tip of Mindanao, two enemy bombers made runs on the destroyer but gunners kept them high and erratic. When *Peary* finally made it to Australia, Fero was

General MacArthur (right) with Major General Jonathan Wainwright, who would become Philippines commander and a prisoner of the Japanese. *Courtesy MacArthur Memorial Library & Archives*

seriously wounded in an air raid on Port Darwin. The Japanese sense of smell had improved.

∞∞∞

AN ANNOUNCEMENT FROM LONDON that the British military had replaced Air Chief Marshal Sir Robert Brooke-Popham with newly arrived Lieutenant General Sir Henry Pownall left little cause for optimism. He had been deputy to General Viscount John Gort in France in 1940 and survived the evacuation of Dunkirk. Although the report suggested that the appointment would "relieve the minds" of pessimists about the future of Singapore, Pownall had an unenviable and brief command. Like Brooke-Popham, a textbook example of military incompetence, before the end he slipped away to England, and to only mild censure. He would assist Churchill in drafting his self-serving postwar memoirs. Only Lieutenant General Sir Arthur Percival would suffer the PM's ignominy of losing Singapore to the Japanese. Unlike Brooke-Popham and Pownall, Percival endured a prison camp. One of his ranking companions there would be General Jonathan Wainwright, to whom MacArthur would leave the Philippines.

IN THE MORNING in Washington Dr. Wilson arrived at the White House by taxi, put a stethoscope to Churchill's chest, and pronounced the incident the night before "nothing serious." Yet both realized that the PM had survived an angina attack. "You have been overdoing things," said Wilson, putting the best face on the matter. He would describe the event in his diary, never revealed until it was published twenty-four years later, just after the PM's death at ninety.

"Now Charles," said Churchill, "you're not going to tell me to rest. I can't. I won't. Nobody else can do this job. I must. What actually happened when I opened the window? My idea is that I strained one of my chest muscles. I used great force. I don't believe it was my heart at all."

"Your circulation is a bit sluggish," Wilson lied, realizing that Churchill was to leave the next day for Ottawa to address the

Canadian Parliament. "You needn't rest in the sense of lying up, but you mustn't do more than you can help in the way of exertion for a little while."

A knock on the door abruptly ended the consultation. It was Harry Hopkins. Wilson edged away with his medical bag into a room where White House secretaries were working and opened a newspaper in semiconcealment. The morning *New York Times* headlined erroneously, "TANK BATTLE SOUTH OF MANILA, LOSSES HEAVY. NEW ENEMY FORCE 175 MILES ABOVE SINGAPORE. CHURCHILL PREDICTS HUGE ALLIED DRIVE IN 1943." Only the last was close to being accurate. However outnumbered, the Japanese in Malaya were moving at will against demoralized defenders who put up only faltering resistance; and in Luzon MacArthur's self-composed communiqués suggested stiff resistance and tank encounters that were only imaginative.

Churchill intimated nothing to Hopkins, who may have assumed that Wilson's visit was routine. "I did not like it," Wilson wrote of his complicity, "but I determined to tell no one." Much later (1984) a physician explained to Churchill's biographer, Martin Gilbert, "The course adopted by Moran [Charles McMoran Wilson became Baron Moran in 1943] on this occasion was quite correct. To have ordered bed rest for six weeks would not have been good therapy as there is no evidence that this does the patient any good and only tends to make them neurotic."

NOT IN DR. WILSON'S NEWSPAPERS nor in print anywhere else was a conversation between Fritz Todt, Hitler's armaments minister, the civil engineering expert who had built Germany's state-of-the-art motorways and was also supervising the construction of an "Atlantic Wall" against the West, and Albert Speer, the Führer's architect and Todt's deputy. "I went to see Todt at his house near Berchtesgaden," Speer recalled. "Given his exalted position it was a very modest place. . . . He was very depressed that day. He was just back from a long inspection trip to Russia, and he told me how horrified he was by the condition of our soldiers." Early winter weather, Todt mourned, had turned Russian roads, never much good anyway, into snowbanks and quagmires. He was ordering workers on *Autobahnen* in Germany to put aside their equipment and go east to repair and maintain the Russian road net. The railways, he added, were impeded by snow and poor trackage, and he had seen for himself "stalled hospital trains in which the wounded had frozen to death, and witnessed the misery of the troops in villages and hamlets cut off by the snow and cold."

Todt confessed that he didn't see how the war could be won. "The Russian soldiers were perhaps primitive, but they were both physically and psychologically much harder than we were. I remember trying to encourage him. Our boys were pretty strong, I said. He shook his head in that special way he had and said— I can still hear him—'You are young. You still have illusions.'" Speer was thirty-six; Todt was a burned-out fifty.

Todt assigned logistics in the Ukraine to Speer who, reluctantly, would make his first visit, to the rubble-strewn industrial city and rail hub of Dnepropetrovsk, late in January, on a Heinkel bomber. Speer left—he thought it was safer—on a crowded hospital train. Todt would not oversee much more. He died on February 8 in the crash of a passenger-converted Heinkel III. Speer would be Todt's successor.

⬯

THE WEEKLY ISSUE of *Time* dated December 27, in the mail or already delivered, described how the American West was responding to the war, with the Pacific Coast newly "conscious of its own immensity." A column reported "a hand-scrawled sign on the fence post of a cross-roads farm: come in for coffee and cake. There were any number of signs like it. . . . Soldiers stationed nearby, passing along the gravel roads, miles from nowhere in the middle of winter, saw them even when they could not stop. . . . In the West, where the war seemed nearer, where the whole region was a military area and where, outside the cities, the line between the soldiers and the people dissolved and all but disappeared in the countryside of scattered farms, small towns, big trees and rain." Concerned that the Japanese who struck Pearl Harbor might come back, "At forest-fire lookout towers, in little tarpaper-covered shacks scattered in hills along the coast, spotters watched the grey skies, 24 hours a day, 24 hours a day, in three-hour shifts. . . . On Whidbey Island in Puget Sound, on the channel in Bremerton, farmers kept watch all night on volunteer beach patrols, moved into shacks when the wind blew down their tents, tending cows when not on patrol."

<hr />

AT THE WHITE HOUSE at 10:00 A.M., Stimson proposed that a joint Southeast Pacific command base be built up "sufficiently far back to be unmolested," suggesting an area beyond likely seizure by the Japanese. Without mentioning Australia, it was clearly the site he had in mind. (Hoping for a more hands-on role for himself, Churchill had proposed instead a "Central Governing Body in Washington" to direct action in the Far East.) Marshall, Stimson, and Arnold all objected to Washington because of the time lag that distance would create. In Arnold's words, "Twenty-four hours would be too late."

Churchill, although tipped off by Hopkins, professed surprise at the suggestion of Wavell as joint commander. Roosevelt also proposed MacArthur—if available—although FDR conceded that no American had sufficient war experience to be "suitable for the post." Arnold offered to "get MacArthur out of the Philippines" if he were the choice. Pride, however, dictated that MacArthur would remain where he was, as he refused to accept from his isolation on Corregidor that he had already lost the Philippines. Ignoring the news from beyond the Rock, about which he knew only from radio, he chose to believe encouraging if unrealistic resupply rhetoric from Marshall and Roosevelt and expected reinforcements to press through the Pacific and repel Japanese seaborne forces blocking shipping lanes toward Luzon. Assistance was indeed on the way—but slowly and obliquely and inadequately. Most of it would stop in Australia and remain there.

The dearth of alternatives left the conferees determined "to start out with Wavell" but—in deference to Churchill—to leave the sea dimension as it was. (The exclusion would not survive future sessions.) Arnold's minutes recorded, with Australia obviously meant but unidentified, "One of the thoughts . . . accepted by all was that we must build up as soon as possible a base in the Far East from which we can gradually move northward, step by step, meeting the Japanese on better than even terms at each step, until ultimately sooner or later we drive the Japanese back from all their present conquests." He might have written "present and future," for the worst was yet to come.

Marshall's proposal of Wavell would leave the British participants vocally worried about public opinion in the United States if events proved, as likely, disastrous, but Churchill contended that Britain should not "shirk the responsibility offered to us" and as a counterweight suggested that naval affairs be under American command in cooperation with General Wavell. Curiously,

Australia itself, beyond Darwin, would be in all practical matters outside Wavell's sphere of control, and his base in India would be given over to an acting deputy. With Japanese advances everywhere, Wavell would oversee a fluctuating and shrinking command and find the reality impossible. He would not last long in his dubious position, which the Japanese would quickly diminish and which officially dissolved on February 25, but the fact of such an appointment initiated what would be a global allied command structure.

As Stimson, Marshall, and Arnold prepared to leave the meeting, with Marshall agreeing to draft a directive to the proposed theater commander, Roosevelt asked Arnold to remain. The general had told him of his conversation the evening before with Lord Beaverbrook (whom *Time* called "dumpy and testy") about war production, particularly the cautious aircraft estimates, Arnold's area of expertise. The American population, with far fewer men under arms, was three times as numerous as Britain. What did Arnold think of the anomaly?

Arnold advised the President that without a collective will to reach industrial potential, Americans could not surpass British production. Still, Arnold cited a promising example. The Boeing factories expected to produce 37 B-17 bombers a month actually completed 50 and would reach 75 in January. More like that could be accomplished elsewhere. According to Arnold's minutes of the conversation, "The President seemed to be greatly pleased by that." In 1940 after the fall of France, Roosevelt had called for an annual production of 50,000 planes, yet implementation by a parsimonious prewar Congress had been sluggish. At the time of Pearl Harbor, the army in Hawaii had only 231 aircraft, half of them obsolete.

IN KENTUCKY AT 10:30 A.M. a B&O train pulled into Louis-ville Station. Waiting on the platform for the sleeper car *Eastlake* were four Secret Service men and a troop from the 13th Armored Division. Verner W. Clapp, chief assistant librarian, who had been aboard, watched over the unloading. The document containers from Washington were lifted into an army truck. Led by a scout vehicle and followed by a car with the four agents, the convoy entered Fort Knox. The cargo was checked in by the chief clerk at the Bullion Depository and placed in Compartment No. 24 on the ground level. The vault was closed at 12:07 P.M. It would not be reopened until late in 1944, for return of the Declaration of Independence, the Constitution, the Bill of Rights, and other founding manuscripts to the Library of Congress.

CHURCHILL AND FDR had lunch at one with Ambassador Litvi-nov at the White House, the subject the joint allied declaration—carefully worded, as Russia was not at war with Japan—on allied unity and goals. Litvinov thought that his government would object to a reference to "freedom of religion" but might accept "freedom of conscience." It was the Christmas season, but the holiday hardly existed in Stalin's domains. Roosevelt altered the term to "religious freedom," which Litvinov suggested might work. He would try it on Moscow.

Just before the afternoon meetings of the chiefs of staff without FDR and Churchill and the luncheon with Litvinov, the President and Prime Minister had met at noon in the Red Room with the heads of diplomatic missions in Washington of nations at war with the Axis powers. The draft declaration of allied unity and aims was under review, in various translations, for each nation to subscribe if acceptable. "We are all in the same boat," said the President, "just as we are all in this room." According to the Mexican ambassador, Castillo Nájera, "The entire interview, from the time of entering the Red Room to the time of departure, lasted thirty-eight minutes." Churchill cabled Deputy Prime Minister Clement Attlee extravagantly, "Today for five hours President and I received representatives of all the other Allied or friendly Powers and British Dominions, and made heartening statements to them." It would lead, within the week, to the declaration initiating the United Nations.

ALTHOUGH DWIGHT EISENHOWER was only assistant chief of the war plans division of army headquarters, Marshall, confident in his new man on the job, was pitching matters large and small to him. To an old West Point friend, Brigadier General LeRoy Lutes, Ike wrote of the "mad house" the War Department had become during the nearly nonstop "Arcadia Conference." Although it was already eight o'clock in the evening and a Sunday, he told Lutes, who was director of operations in the Services of Supply and who would several years later be Ike's logistics deputy, "I have a couple of hours' work ahead of me, and tomorrow will be no different from today. I have been here about three weeks and this noon had my first luncheon outside of the office. Usually it is a hot-dog sandwich and a glass of milk. I have had one evening meal in the whole period."

Eisenhower bedded temporarily in Virginia at "Tall Oaks," his brother Milton's posh estate (Helen Eakin's family was prosperous) in Falls Church. "Every night when I reached their house, regardless of the hour, which averaged something around midnight," Ike recalled, "both would be waiting up for me with a snack of midnight supper and a pot of coffee. I cannot remember ever seeing their house in daylight." Putting in sixteen-hour days, he was picked up by an army staff car heading for the Potomac bridges before the winter sun arose. Barely visible in the wan light were billboards importuning, "WAR WORKERS NEED ROOMS, APARTMENTS, HOMES. REGISTER YOUR VACANCIES NOW." He too would need one when Mamie relocated from Texas.

The day before, Major General "Vinegar Joe" Stilwell had written to his wife about the frenzied activity in the War Department. A veteran of combat in France in 1918, he had been summoned by Marshall from command of III Corps to direct the possible invasion of Vichy North Africa. "My impression of Washington," he wrote, "is a rush of clerks in and out of doors, swing doors always swinging, people with papers rushing after other people with papers, groups in corners whispering in huddles, everybody jumping up just as you start to talk, buzzers ringing, telephones ringing, rooms crowded, with clerks all banging away at typewriters. . . . Everybody furiously smoking cigarettes, everybody passing you on the way to someone else. . . ." His hurried relocation would quickly lead to nothing. Shortages of shipping everywhere made North Africa a present impossibility. Marshall estimated to the British that the operation was at least "three months away"—at that an unrealistic estimate of a venture that would take place the next November.

That Saturday afternoon at 3:00 P.M. the entire military leadership on both sides, including a secretariat of six, filed into a conference room in the Federal Reserve Building. Again the North African operation came up, and Air Marshal Portal confessed that he was "horrified at the large number of planes contemplated." He called for a "spirit of economy," and with the apparent aim of killing the venture, Arnold recommended referring the proposal to the Joint Planning Committee. Marshall had still another tactic to bury Portal's bare bones idea. If the means were insufficient to guarantee success, he wanted no part in it.

The operation might be "the first contact between American and German troops. . . . A failure in this first venture would have an extremely adverse effect on the morale of the American people."

With North Africa unsettled yet increasingly unlikely in the immediate future, the conferees turned to the Far East theater and the unity of command that still seemed unsettled, which meant taking up the draft directive Marshall had prepared for the unnamed designee. Like Churchill although not speaking for him, Admiral Dudley Pound spoke of his doubts at having a general oversee "naval matters." Marshall, who had already countered the PM's concerns about an all-purpose commander, said that he assumed that "a man of good judgment," from whatever service, would be selected and that bolstered by unity of command, he would have "a distinct advantage over a man with brilliant judgment who must rely [only] on cooperation." He read his frank directive and had copies distributed, remarking that the "Associated Powers" were opposing "an enemy who has unity of command in its highest sense. . . . The situation in this respect could not be made worse that it exists at present." It was "tragic."

On reading the draft Field Marshal Dill, who would become a close, valued friend of Marshall's through the war, described it as "a good basis to work on, but the restrictions would make it very difficult for the Commander-in-Chief to exercise command." Marshall conceded the restrictions, adding that "if the Supreme Commander ended up with no more authority than to tell Washington what he wanted, such a situation was better than nothing, and an improvement over the present situation." Portal then commended the directive for its "realism" but questioned whether it would be possible "to give the commander a free hand, and to have all the political questions resolved, say, in Washington, or, as an alternative . . . , a representative in the area?"

Marshall stood firm on limiting only political questions to review by a War Council in Washington. Employing a distant surrogate for military matters was inefficient "idealism." What he wanted was "to start something." And that policy was agreed upon "in broad outline," with "the details worked out later." The President asked Marshall and Hopkins to "retire" to another room and revise the proposal for unification to include Churchill's views about protecting local "sovereign rights," such as those of the Dutch and the Australians, but he clearly implied British colonial interests as well. Naval forces, all now agreed, would be placed under the supreme commander to be designated.

Although Churchill still had misgivings, the unity issue was almost settled. When the conference adjourned at 4:30 P.M., Marshall recalled in an interview fifteen years later, "I got up and started down the steps and Dill reached me at the top of the steps. No, the first man to reach me was the old admiral [Dudley Pound] who was the head of the naval board—[both] which were pretty cut and dried fellows and more or less opposed to all of this—and he embraced me to my complete astonishment. Dill [also] met me and embraced me. . . . So then Hopkins heard of this and he suggested to Churchill that he get [to see] me in the next morning." The military chiefs had come around. Lord Beaverbrook scrawled a note to Hopkins on a White House memo pad, "You should work on Churchill. He is being advised. He is open-minded and needs discussion." The Beaver had also come around.

At the White House at six, Roosevelt and Churchill met with their foreign affairs advisers; then Hull had dinner separately with Mackenzie King on the trifling French imbroglio. On larger issues, Dr. Wilson thought, as sounding board for Churchill's confidences, "Marshall remains the key to the situation. The PM has a feeling in his quiet unprovocative way he means business, and that if we are too obstinate he might take a strong[er] line. And neither the PM nor the President can contemplate going forward without Marshall."

December 28, 1941

As *Peary* neared Celebes (now Sulawesi) en route toward Manado on the northern tentacle of the scorpion-shaped Indonesian island, three twin-engine bombers were sighted approaching from astern. According to the ship's log, battle stations were manned,

and as the planes made a bombing approach, *Peary* opened fire. Fire was stopped when British [Australian] markings were observed on the wings. The planes had separated, one each, taking station on the port and starboard bow and one eastern. The plane astern made a bombing run and dropped two bombs about fifty yards astern as *Peary* kicked ahead at full [power]. *Peary* again slowed and the plane on the port bow made her approach simultaneously with the other. *Peary* leaped forward, opening fire with machine guns and 4" [battery]. Sights were set at zero deflection and 500 yds range. One plane dropped two bombs near the port bow and the starboard plane dropped two about 25 yds from the stern. Shrapnel damage was extensive. One machine gunner on the makeshift director platform[, Seaman K. E. Quineaux, a French Canadian,] was killed instantly with a head wound. He had been directly over [Lt. W. J.] Catlett, who was navigating from the port wing. The bombs aft, severed the wheel ropes to the rudder and split open two depth charges, in addition to wounding two men. The planes flew away and made [return] strafing machine gun runs. *Peary* set up an intense fire curtain with her machine guns and 4" battery. At this time, the cry "Man Overboard" went up but *Peary* had to continue her evasive tactics from the strafing runs, and leave the man to shift for himself.

Fireman B. E. Greene, one of the walking wounded at Cavite, manning the afterdeck house machine gun, had toppled overboard as the *Peary*'s stern whipped about. Radioman H. D. Doe, one of Admiral Hart's "Purple gang," stationed as a lookout with Greene, threw him a life ring and reported that when last seen he was swimming, in his life jacket, with the ring, toward the beach half a mile distant. Several small boats were seen "putting out from the beach." Greene survived in Dutch hands.

In the heat of action against what the crew recognized as RAAF Lockheed Hudsons, light bombers based upon the ten-passenger civilian Electra, Radioman Doe had not known that he had shrapnel wounds to his forehead and both buttocks. "He now realized that it was not water splashes, which gave him a wet behind. He let his pants down and reassured himself that the importants were in order." One seaman in the gun crew surveyed Doe's shrapnel lacerations and joked, "How do you put a tourniquet on a rear end without putting pressure on his balls?" Radioman Doe was placed, face down, on the deck until a mattress could be brought up to carry him to the ship's "Doc." He was grateful for the padding: "This damned deck vibrates so much, I'll lose my teeth."

"All hands," according to the log, "behaved in an exemplary manner, as they should, being professionals. Many little acts of heroism took place as natural, trained reactions." When Fireman M. E. Fryman of the damage control group wanted to throw over the side a damaged but unexploded white phosphorus star shell in its flaming wooden container, he held it until the stern of *Peary* whipped about so that he could heave it clear of the ship's propeller. It was a "fearsome thing to wrap one's arms about, and wait."

The damage and the casualties were due to misnamed "friendly fire," the bane of warfare. *Peary*'s jury-rigged antennas, patched after the Cavite raids, were now nearly useless. The ship had code experts aboard "but could not effectively communicate." Its ability to steer from the bridge was gone. The hull at the engine room had twenty punctures. It had lost a .30-caliber Lewis gun. And its attackers were "planes made in America." Yet it was far from the first—or worst—friendly fire episode since Pearl Harbor. Six carrier planes from the *Enterprise,* at sea, flying in after the Japanese had left, were mistaken for the enemy by panicky gunners on Oahu who did not recognize their own identifying markings. This time American fire was accurate and deadly. One pilot, bailing out of his burning "Wildcat" fighter, was shot in the chest as he drifted down.

Friendly fire was always a nightmare in the fog of war, often concealed by cover-ups that later unraveled.

WITH MACARTHUR HOLED UP on Corregidor and all of the Philippines doomed, the Japanese were beginning to exploit collaborators to create a vassal nation. Radioing Washington, MacArthur urged countering, somehow, the "crescendo of enemy propaganda" which was being used with "deadly effectiveness." In a rare confession he added, "I am not in a position here to combat it." In response, Roosevelt drafted a proclamation directed to the people of the Philippines and meant for radio there as well as domestic airing in the United States. "I renew my solemn pledge to you," the President declared, "that your freedom will be redeemed and your independence established and protected." *Redeemed* suggested the obvious. The Philippines were being lost—but not yet sufficiently lost for MacArthur to abandon his personal priorities. From Corregidor, which had an under-the-bay cable to Malacañag, the nearly abandoned presidential palace in Manila, the general telephoned Jorge Vargas. "Jorge," he explained, "I have not yet taken the 70,000 [Philippines pesos] contingency fund that is due me."

"What do you want me to do, General?" asked the surprised Vargas, who had been left to administer the last rites to the government.

"Can you buy me $35,000 worth of Lepanto [gold-mining] stocks?" MacArthur inquired.

"We will try, General; we will try," assured Vargas. He struggled by transoceanic telephone to locate the manager of the Philippine National Bank's New York office. "After the war," said Vargas, released from Sugamo Prison in Tokyo, "MacArthur became a millionaire on account of that last-minute purchase." The general was comfortably wealthy far earlier than 1941, but even amid catastrophe he looked for ways to pad his portfolio.

Free to enter Manila unopposed, General Homma preferred to consolidate his lines, north and south, to pinch off any possible resistance on Luzon beyond Bataan, but the result was to leave the peninsula open for further withdrawals into it. Homma was taking few prisoners, as able Americans and Filipinos were falling back into their last-ditch positions in such tightly packed numbers, swelled by refugees, as to further overwhelm their diminishing food supplies and ammunition. It may not have been the general's strategic objective, but at little cost in his own casualties Homma was creating a starve-out dilemma for the defense.

TWO CONVOYS LEFT BRISBANE for northern ports. The *Pensacola* group, which had arrived on the 22nd from Hawaii, headed for Darwin to help secure it from the Japanese. Ostensibly it was still tasked to support the Philippines, but no effort would be made to risk that. (One battalion aboard from the 131st Field Artillery would be sent uselessly to Java, where its remnants would be taken prisoner in March.) The same day the American cruiser *Houston* with four destroyers as support vessels would also arrive, soon to join a Dutch-commanded force which would fail to hold off the invasion of Java. (The *Houston,* with other warships, would be bombed to the bottom of the Sunda Strait on March 1.) Sailing northeast was a British force, including the 44,786-ton former passenger liner *Acquitania,* en route to Port Moresby, New Guinea, with five thousand Australian troops intended to prevent the major harbor on the big island from falling into enemy hands. Port Moresby would become a major staging area.

THE DAYS ELSEWHERE made no difference to Anthony Eden's voyage from frigid Murmansk, other than that each revolution of the clock brought the endangered convoy farther from chances of German air or submarine attacks. "Bitter weather—somewhere off Fa[e]roes," Oliver Harvey wrote. The island group, a Danish colony between Iceland and the Shetland Islands and now under British occupation, was distant enough from German bases in Norway to offer some safety but was often closed in by fog and rain. "Fairly nice day and a little sun—stayed on the bridge a bit," Harvey noted happily. They were still under radio silence but could receive news and messages. "After lunch [I] talked with A.E. about what he should say to press on arrival and also on his [BBC] broadcast. He is a little jealous of Winston with all his limelight in Washington but feels, as I do, that he talks too much. An officer of the ship spoke to me today of his speech [to Congress] as 'so much soap.' No harm therefore in A.E. sitting pretty and getting on with the [foreign affairs] job." Eden and his staff had to turn water into wine.

⌒⌒⌒

CHURCHILL WAS TO LEAVE Washington for Canada later in the day. The PM's laid-back managerial style was often literal. His first meeting, Marshall told Eisenhower, "took place at nine-o'clock . . . in Mr. Churchill's bedroom. . . . The Prime Minister was propped up in bed with his work board resting against his knees and the usual cigar in his mouth or swung like a baton to emphasize his points." Nearly five years later, when Churchill came to a postwar Conservative Party conference in the home-town of Paul Johnson, the aspiring historian, then sixteen and without adult inhibitions, slipped close and asked, "Mr. Winston Churchill, to what do you attribute your success in life?"

"Conservation of energy," said Churchill. "Never stand up when you can sit down. And never sit down when you can lie down."

With Marshall, the PM, from bed, discussed the almost-settled issue of unity of command in Southeast Asia. Although even his senior admiral in the conference had conceded the issue, Churchill was unconvinced about including naval forces. "What would an army officer know about handling a ship?" he challenged. Although Wavell was Churchill's own man, he did not want a general—even a field marshal—commanding the Royal Navy anywhere.

"Well," said Marshall, who was never less than direct, "what the devil does a naval officer know about handling a tank?" The problem, he contended, was not about sailors or tankers but about "getting control." When Churchill resorted to the history books, Marshall said he was not interested in the bygone era of Drake and Frobisher but "in having a united front against Japan. . . . If we didn't do something right away, we were finished in the war." His directive, he went on, was "to meet the onrush of the Japanese in the South Pacific, where they were overwhelming an ill-prepared, pitifully equipped collection of British-Australians, Indian[s] and Indonese, Americans and New Zealanders. . . ." Someone had to be in charge, and that someone did not have to be "an expert in all the particulars." Roosevelt, he added, had overall responsibility for the American war effort, "and he doesn't know about any of it." To his sister, Marshall wrote, exasperated, of the "so-called holidays."

Worn down, Churchill drafted a cable to the Cabinet in London, agreeing "provisionally" with the proposal as "strongly endorsed by General Marshall." It would be the precedent for all Allied theater commands throughout the war. In square miles the ABDA theater from Burma to Australia was as large as the United States, and its military unity was largely rhetorical. In his diary Eisenhower wrote impatiently, "Good start! But what an effort. Talk-talk-talk." Yet it proved more than talk, and Eisenhower himself would receive one of the commands, and then another.

⚬⚬⚬

THE PRESIDENT MET with his service advisers and the ubiquitous Hopkins at 11:45 A.M. Admiral King reported that the first naval priority was protecting the line between Hawaii and Midway Island, with the second priority of safeguarding the supply line from Hawaii through Samoa to Australia. Roosevelt asked about the possibility of "some kind of contact with the Japanese navy" so that Americans would feel that withdrawals were not the only option, and he asked Marshall about sending troops in small batches to Britain "on current convoys." FDR also wanted several freighters about to be converted to escort aircraft carriers rescheduled for refitting as troop transports. He wanted to say something publicly—he was thinking of his State of the Union address to Congress on January 6—about American forces taking "stations" in the British Isles. And he termed the proposed North African venture "a guess operation." Agreeing, Marshall again warned that a premature landing under Vichy French fire at Casablanca might meet "an initial reverse which would have a very detrimental effect on the morale of the American people."

Much remained to be done before Churchill traveled to Ottawa for the address to Parliament. Roosevelt had arranged to have his presidential Pullman car, the *Ferdinand Magellan,* attached, for the PM's comfort, to the returning Canadian train. Churchill would travel with his physician, valet, Air Chief Marshal Portal, a security detail, and secretaries. The rest of the British party would remain for continued discussions.

Other working meetings dealt with dismal prospects. Even in North Africa, where General Auchinleck's Eighth Army seemed to be moving relentlessly along the Libyan coast, General Rommel's resupplied Afrika Korps counterattacked, sending the survivors of the surprised 22nd Armoured Brigade into retreat. The Japanese had landed a small force near Davao on the big southern island of Mindanao, second largest in the Philippines. MacArthur radioed Washington from his isolated headquarters on Corregidor that, although he had evacuated his remaining B-17 bombers to Java, he hoped to hold on to airfields in Mindanao to protect the inner islands of the Philippines. It was an empty prospect because the eighteen additional B-17s that Marshall announced would be leaving for the Far East the next day, far short of the clouds of planes needed but yet unbuilt, had no likelihood of being flown from Australia for missions from doomed Mindanao.

That Manila had been declared an open city and remained undefended did not restrain the Japanese from bombing suspected military targets. Formerly isolationist senator Burton K. Wheeler of Montana vowed nevertheless that the "Japs will pay" for the outrages. To MacArthur came an encouraging but unrealistic radio message from Marshall that "the President [has] personally directed the Navy to make every effort to support you. You can rest assured [that] War Department will do all in its power to build up at top speed air power in Far East to completely dominate that region." However, the promise had a long fuse, and Marshall—privately—considered MacArthur effectively "a prisoner on Corregidor."

BEFORE CHURCHILL ENTRAINED for Canada he met with FDR and Secretary of State Hull about the Gaullist seizure of St. Pierre and Miquelon, which impaired already difficult relations with the Vichy French. Hull referred to the "so-called Free French" and called the haughty de Gaulle "a marplot acting directly contrary to the expressed wishes of Britain, Canada, and the United States." Trivializing the episode in drafting his postwar memoirs, Churchill claimed that Hull, "for whom I entertained the highest respect" (which was untrue), had "pushed what was little more than a departmental point far beyond its proportions." He kept that in but excised his charge that Hull cut "a rather pathetic figure" about an incident that "did not enter at all into our main discussions." Yet it had. Churchill warned that forcing out the Gaullists would impair his fragile relations with the Free French movement. Roosevelt and Hull wanted to retain ties with Vichy, as a sizeable French fleet still remained out of Nazi hands. It was not the only cause of friction, as the discussions covered the world. Churchill was trying to preserve an empire that would never again be as it was, while Roosevelt saw the disintegrating British colonial anachronism as unworthy of saving.

Informed by the PM that he had to accept the already fraying ABDA appointment, Wavell responded to Field Marshal Dill that he hoped no announcement would be made before he received his instructions. When Dill radioed a summary, Wavell responded that he felt that he had been left not holding the baby, but quadruplets. Although his official appointment would not arrive from Washington until January 3, the BBC and the Australian press had already announced it.

CHURCHILL DEPARTED LATE that afternoon for the overnight trip to Ottawa, dictating and receiving cables and making telephone calls en route. He cabled Australian Prime Minister John Curtin about the appointment of Wavell, with American army air forces major general George H. Brett as his deputy and an "appropriate joint body" in Washington to oversee affairs. "The decision has come from them," Churchill explained. "I have not attempted to argue the case for or against accepting this broadminded and selfless American proposal, of [the] merits of which as a war winner I have become convinced. Action is urgent. . . ." There would be another South Pacific area theater, he predicted, including most of Australia, under an American commander.

In Washington, when Hopkins reported the difficulties with the Australian government in accepting an imposed ABDA command, with all but the northern rim of the island continent excluded, Marshall recommended that Australian and New Zealand representatives in Washington be involved in further "joint" arrangements—the "sovereign rights" aspect. Visualizing an American umbrella, the Australian government quickly accepted. Despite the country's vastness, it had almost no air force, a very small navy, and an army largely overseas and at great hazard, augmenting the British in Libya and also in Singapore— where many Aussie survivors ended up as prisoners of war building the bridge on the River Kwai.

UNKNOWN TO ALL, an unreported episode in occupied Europe, "Operation Arthropoid," would have repercussions months later. An RAF Halifax bomber at 10:00 P.M. Berlin time, which was mandated for occupied Czechoslovakia, dropped Jan Kubiš and Jozef Gabčík, with seven soldiers from the Czech army-in-exile, by parachute near what pilots thought was Pilsen but was actually Nehvizdy, east of Prague. Their mission was to assassinate the notorious Nazi overseer of Bohemia and Moravia (Slovakia was split off into a puppet state), Reinhard Heydrich. Although his blood-stained reputation was well known, his most newsworthy act of the week was to order a statue of wartime President Woodrow Wilson, a gift of American Czechs in 1928, removed from its place in front of Prague's central railway station. As a gesture of quiet defiance, local citizens had been placing flowers at its base. Hiding in safe houses and on the run, the conspirators after the Reich Protector would finally catch up to him on May 27, 1942, throwing an antitank grenade into his open Mercedes-Benz. After Heydrich died of shrapnel wounds in Prague seven days later, Hitler ordered the SS and Gestapo to "wade in blood"

to find the killers. Thousands were arrested. Kubiš was killed in a gun battle; Gabčík committed suicide rather than be captured; the village of Lidice was destroyed in reprisal and all 199 male residents executed. Weighing the price of reprisals, Churchill would order a halt to further plans to kill high-ranking Nazis.

As the PM left the White House with Dr. Wilson for Union Station (Mackenzie King traveled in a separate vehicle as did Churchill's staff), he rolled down the window of his car, claiming that he was short of breath. "There seems no air in this car. Is it a stuffy night, Charles?" He put his hand on Wilson's knee, saying, "It is a great comfort to have you with me." The emotional effect of his heart seizure lingered.

Dinner hour at 7:30 found Roosevelt and Hopkins in their beds, exhausted. A butler reported, "Theys flat out in bed eating off trays." Eleanor had concocted scrambled eggs, the first time she had done so since the hectic evening of Pearl Harbor.

December 29, 1941

Although some destroyers in Division 59 had weighed anchor and left Surabaja, *Paul Jones* and *Barker* remained, and *Ford* and *Pope,* damaged at Cavite, were still undergoing "minor overhaul." Ensign Cross managed to create some errands ashore in the morning and "on the way, firmed up the dinner date with the little sales-girls in the jewelry shop. That evening he and [Lt.] Joe Harmon took off on their date. Harmon's 'blind date' was a 'knockout.' They really lucked out in having the two most beautiful girls in Surabaja. The shop was closed and the four took off for the Dutch Naval Officer's Club. There was a bit of commotion when they entered and were shown a table. Finally the Maitrè D went to their table and asked them to leave for the Club's rules specified that only officers and [their] families were to be served." The young women, very likely used to racial exclusion, "took it in stride and they all went to a small, neat café which was familiar to the girls and the four had a delightful time, with music, dancing, a few drinks. Conversation, etc. The evening ended with the hope that more would follow." (But the destroyers soon departed. Harmon, later to become a navy pilot, would be killed in action flying an F6F "Hellcat" fighter.)

Victimized by friendly fire, *Peary* remained in mechanical trouble, continuing underway east of Celebes in early morning darkness with only one screw, yet making twenty-two knots.

With steering from the bridge gone, the navigator called out directions to the captain on the afterdeck. Mooring between two Dutch islands in the Moluccan Sea group, the crew at daybreak lowered a motor whaleboat to the beach. At cone-dominated, volcanic Ternate they found "medical people" to treat the wounded while shipfitters welded and patched shrapnel holes in the stern. Seamen gathered large palm leaves to conceal the deck and blend in with the shoreline. Another trip in brought "lots of beer, bread and fresh fruit, and for the officers and CPOs some excellent Dutch rum." A landing force brought to shore

> plenty of mosquito nets . . . to ward off the large ants and mosquito[e]s. As lush fruit trees extended to the water's edge, Chief Pharmacist's Mate [Ed] Parker, with the Captain's blessing, urged the men to get as much rest as possible and also pointed out that the last few days and nights had undoubtedly tightened up their guts, that the remedy . . . was close at hand, with all the mangoes. . . . All hands scattered, eating all the while and then gathering [fruit] for the future. The way the men buried their faces into the pink flesh of the mangoes until the juices ran down their mostly naked chests forecast, relative to Parker's fear of constipation problems, [that] it would soon disappear. In anticipation, a small latrine area was dug.

Dutch settlers hoped that that *Peary* would remain and defend them, but all that Lieutenant Bermingham could do—his orders were for Darwin—was to turn over fifteen rifles, four Browning ("BAR") automatic rifles, and four boxes of ammunition—4,800 rounds—to cope with the Japanese. *Peary*'s presence, Bermingham explained, was their real danger. A radio station high on a hill overlooking the ship overheard and reported that a Japanese landing attempt at Manado, from an offshore cruiser, had been turned away. (Manado, across the Moluccan Sea, would be attacked again, and occupied, on January 11. Ternate's pathetic defenses would soon be useless.)

When two planes overhead that afternoon appeared to be Navy PBY reconnaissance craft, Bermingham ordered out the whaleboat into open water to flag them down, and he described to the airmen the friendly fire attack by the RAAF the day before. One of the pilots suggested that the *Peary*'s jury-rigged topside after the Cavite raid altered its recognition-book appearance from overhead and promised to return the next day to lead the ship out, skimming the surface for a distance to avoid giving away its location. Bermingham then ordered all fresh water use aboard cut off and men to wash themselves and their clothes at the beach. Lieutenant M. M. Kovisto, the executive officer, called the men to attention in order to hold a burial service for Seaman Quineaux, after which the captain eulogized the French-Canadian's love of his adopted country. A sailor who died at sea by custom should be buried at sea. Weights, a line, and the body were placed on a canvas stretcher and stowed in the bow of the whaleboat. Bermingham "and a six-man firing squad embarked and the MWB went out to the end of the deep channel. After three volleys, the body was consigned to the deep."

FROM LATERAL #3, one of the branch tunnels carved into the rock of Corregidor, where MacArthur now had a desk and makeshift headquarters, he drafted an urgent order to commandeer supplies for Bataan, which had been disastrously neglected both in peace and in war. Huge stocks of everything that might have been useful had been neglected, then left onshore to looters and the enemy. A few supply officers instructed to remain at Intramuros until the Japanese closed in hired barges and boats to haul food to Bataan yet were under contradictory orders from MacArthur to leave sufficient quantities for the population of Manila. In the central Luzon plain, at Cabanatuan, with no transport available, 4,500 tons of rice, enough to feed the 105,000 soldiers and refugees on Bataan for five months, had been abandoned to the Japanese, as well as 3,400,000 gallons of fuel and a half-million rounds of rifle ammunition. Barely days later, troops on Bataan were on short rations and even low in potable water.

Just before noon enemy bombers began raiding Topside. Fleeing residents, including Arthur and Jean MacArthur, huddled in

Jean MacArthur with the general after their evacuation to Corregidor. *Courtesy MacArthur Memorial Library & Archives*

a tunnel for three and a half hours while the general, refusing to wear a helmet, watched his house of several days collapse, and as the wreckage scattered and watchers flattened themselves to the ground, a Filipino soldier took off his own helmet and held it over MacArthur's head. The general was unscathed, but Sergeant Domingo Adversario took a small shrapnel hit to his hand. MacArthur would award him a Purple Heart and a Silver Star, the beginning of his wholesale decoration of troops—and his inner circle.

IN MALAYA the Japanese began assaulting Kuantan on the eastern coast, almost parallel to Kuala Lumpur on the other side of the Kra Peninsula. A brigade of the 9th Indian Division, protecting cratered airfields that had no usable planes, fought them off until their British commander was taken prisoner. Then what was left of the brigade surrendered. "Why did your men raise their hands so quickly?" he was asked.

As Colonel Tsuji reported (in a somewhat stilted translation), the British officer explained, "When we defend the coast, you come from the dense jungle. When we defend the land, you come from the sea. Is it not war for enemies to face each other? This is not war. There will be no other way than retreat. . . ."

RETREAT WAS ALSO ON THE MIND of harried General Halder, who saw no other solution on the vast Russian front. "A very bad day!" he began his diary for December 29. In the Crimea, Count Hans von Sponeck, commanding, had withdrawn the

46th Division from the Kerch Peninsula "under the first shock of an enemy landing. . . . He has immediately been removed from his post, but the damage done can hardly be repaired." In Army Group Center, in snow and ice,

> the enemy's superiority on the fronts of the Second Army and Second Panzer Army is beginning to tell. We did succeed in sealing the penetrations, but the situation on the overextended front, at which the enemy keeps hammering with ever new concentrations, is very difficult in view of the exhaustion of our troops. . . . The bulk of the enemy is advancing unchecked in the direction of Yukhnov (paratroop landings!). Kaluga and the salient to the north must be abandoned in order to collect forces strong enough to stem the enemy breakthrough across the Oka. On the army front to the north, partly heavy fighting resulting in enemy penetrations.

Everywhere on the Russian front in the north, after successive enemy breakthroughs "the army line had to be taken farther back again"—Halder's euphemism for withdrawals. "At Führer Hq., dramatic telephone conversations with [Colonel-General] von Richthofen, who temporarily will take over command of VI Corps. . . ." Hitler had relieved yet another general, putting a pragmatic air force general in command of ground troops.

------∞------

STILL AT SEA but in radio listening contact with England, Anthony Eden, according to Oliver Harvey, was "very annoyed at inadequate publicity given to our visit on B.B.C. midnight news." While Churchill was acquiring broadcast time and newspaper headlines, the foreign secretary had been on a far more dangerous mission to a far more difficult allied head of state. Harvey assured Eden that the morning papers will give his return "the fullest treatment but he won't be comforted. He has written a telegram [to his London office] he wants to have sent off as soon as possible. . . . (We can't break wireless silence till midday.) He thinks we should have a photographer and a press officer with us. . . . What a curse publicity is. I can't really feel it matters very much, though it is important that the Russians should not think we don't attach enormous importance to the visit and their hospitality and that the British should also understand this." Useful publicity, he thought, "can't be overdone," but he was getting no cooperation from his traveling colleague, career diplomat Sir Alexander Cadogan—"he just grunts and goes away to bed. 'All prima donnas,' he says."

Ottawa was snow-covered as Mackenzie King's special train pulled into the city just after ten in the morning. Enthusiastic crowds, undaunted by the weather or by the fur-hatted Royal Canadian Mounted Police, swarmed through the station. Among the dignitaries up front was the American ambassador. "There was Mr. Churchill," J. Pierrepont Moffat wrote, "standing on the platform in characteristic pose, puffing a newly lit cigar and holding up his right hand making the sign of V. As the temperature was about zero, introductions on the platform were made on the double quick and he hastened away. . . ."

"We drove to Government House [Rideau Hall] through streets banked with snow," Dr. Wilson noted in his diary. "After a hot bath, Winston seemed his usual self." A lunch with the Canadian War Cabinet at the Château Laurier followed, during which Churchill excused himself to hone his speech for the next day and to worry further to Dr. Wilson about the cardiac episode in the White House. "Whenever we are alone," the exasperated

Wilson noted in his diary, "he keeps asking me to take his pulse. I get out of it somehow, but once, when I found him lifting something heavy, I did expostulate."

"Now, Charles," Churchill said, "you are making me heart-minded. I shall soon think of nothing else. I couldn't do my work if I kept thinking of my heart."

The next time Wilson was asked to check the PM's pulse, he refused. "You're all right," he said. "Forget your damned heart."

WITH WASHINGTON STILL ON HIS MIND and Canadian issues to handle gingerly, Churchill telephoned Harry Hopkins at the White House at 6:45 P.M., who minuted to the President,

> The Prime Minister just phoned me, . . . reading me a cable from the Foreign Office to him, in which they indicate the most strenuous objection to the ousting of the Free French from Miquelon.
>
> They claim that de Gaulle will not issue the orders to throw his commander [Admiral Muselier] out.
>
> The burden of the message was that the whole business would kick up an unbelievable row, for which we could give no good public explanation. In spite of the fact that de Gaulle acted in bad faith, the British don't see how he can be forced out and think that the use of force would be very bad.

Roosevelt's jaundiced view of the general, who had grandly assumed the mantle of France-in-exile and depended entirely on British and American material support but privately referred to his enablers as "foreigners," would never soften, although events to come would require a frosty public correctness on both sides.

THE BRITISH PRESS was playing up Churchill abroad as a one-man show. Clementine wrote to him, "I have been thinking constantly of you & trying to picture & realize the drama in which you are playing the principal—or rather it seems—the only part—I pray that when you leave, that the fervour you have aroused may not die down but will consolidate into practical & far-reaching action." She found the news from Malaya and Sumatra "disquieting" yet knew only what the newspapers could print. "No news of Mary since Christmas Eve when she . . . blew in for a hot bath & a bite of dinner & Sarah is completely swallowed in her W.A.A.F." Daughter Mary was a corporal with an anti-aircraft battery stationed in Hyde Park, and Sarah was an Aircraft Woman Second Class being trained in interpretation of aerial photographs.

IN WASHINGTON Japanese diplomats, watched by Capital police, were still residing in their embassy on Massachusetts Avenue. As the likelihood of rapid exchange with American equivalents in Tokyo dimmed, the government had to lodge them somewhere remote from the capital but not in so dismal a location as to prompt retaliation by Japan. After negotiations with an appropriate hostelry, the diplomats with their families were ordered to be ready to depart on the twenty-ninth. A police motorcycle escort headed a column of four buses, three limousines, and five trucks for baggage, routed to Union Station. There the mission's personnel were put aboard a special train to the Homestead Hotel, a resort in Hot Springs, Virginia, where they were to remain under guard. A gracious hotel in the Allegheny Mountains, complete to golf links, it had little winter business during the month of Pearl Harbor, but the management asked that the State Department guarantee to pay for any damage the Japanese might do and to move them out by April 1, the beginning of the spring season—should there be one. State promised nothing, but however unlikely it had seemed, the Homestead's winter season was suddenly profitable.

The hotel library lacked books which a low-level diplomat, on arrival, wanted. He requested that State supply Albert Schweitzer's *The Quest for the Historical Jesus*—an appropriate title for the Christmas season—Carl Sandburg's *Abraham Lincoln: The War Years,* and the complete works of Shakespeare. He expected a long war and the need to improve his English. A senior diplomat requested vital supplies inadvertently left behind—five cases of Old Paar Scotch and five cases of Johnnie Walker Black Label.

German, Hungarian, and Italian diplomats received equal treatment. They were settled at the Greenbrier Hotel in White Sulphur Springs, West Virginia. The management soon complained that their dogs were ruining the carpets and that their children were roller-skating in the hallways and playing in the elevators. The Italians would dislike being confined with the Germans, and the Germans considered the Italians a "barbaric" people. The State Department would have its own little war to adjudicate.

At the Navy Department a less-than-quiet internal war was also underway. Rear Admiral Kimmel (his four-star rank at Pearl Harbor had been temporary) would soon be home from Hawaii, either to be reassigned or await a worse fate. Admiral Harold R. Stark, the Chief of Naval Operations, was being criticized for prewar timidity but expected to keep his job. He had been a friend of the President since FDR had been assistant secretary of the navy in the earlier world war. "Don't worry about our finding duty for you," Stark reassured Kimmel on the 29th. "I value your services just as much as I ever did and more[,] and I say this straight from the heart as well as the head." Yet Stark's tenure as CNO was in jeopardy, and he would soon be replaced by crusty Admiral Ernest J. King, then Atlantic Fleet commander. Stark would be posted to London, and Kimmel nowhere.*

AT 2:30 P.M. in the office in the Capitol of Vice President Henry A. Wallace, a dozen American officials involved in war production matters met with Lord Beaverbrook, the Minister of Supply. His former brief had limited him to aircraft production. Max Beaverbrook was not overwhelmed by the names or the numbers. Small, balding, and potbellied, he was outsized in other ways. Wallace recalled his "dynamism. . . . He was a power house with regard to what could be done and what had to be done. . . . Some people did not like the Beaver but he stands out in my mind more than anyone else at this particular moment." More than anyone else in Britain, he had cajoled labor and industrialists into meeting production goals they thought were outrageous fantasy, and he found the raw materials and got them delivered in the face of catastrophic sinkings by German subs and massive bombings of factories by the *Luftwaffe*. Taking minutes was Donald Nelson, then Chairman of the War Production Board and former executive vice president of Sears, Roebuck:

---

*Kimmel took early retirement in February 1942 and spent years defending himself.

Lord Beaverbrook emphasized the fact that we must set our production sights much higher than we have for the year 1942, in order that we might cope with a resourceful and determined enemy. He pointed out that we had yet no experience in the losses of materiel incidental to a war of the kind we are now fighting. He also felt we had very little conception of the productive facilities of the Axis powers. He said that . . . Stalin told him that Germany had thrown 30,000 tanks into the fight with Russia, and that starting from scratch as we were we had to build up a reserve in addition to supplying our troops with the necessary tanks to fight. He made the statement that if an invasion . . . were attempted we had no conception of the number of tanks we would have to cope with [on the Continent of Europe]. He emphasized over and over again the fact that we should set our sights higher in planning for production of the necessary war material. For instance, he thinks we should plan for the production of 45,000 tanks in 1942 against Mr. Knudsen's estimate of 30,000.

I want to take up the question of what is preventing us from producing 25,000 medium and 15,000 light tanks per month. [He meant *year*.] I want to check merchant shipping, the conversion factor from dead weight, gross weight and cargo carrying capacity. I want to check the bottlenecks on the 3 inch versus the 57 millimeter gun, the number of man-hours, machinery involved, etc.

Beaverbrook's tank example was applied to everything war-expendable in the national armory, from airplanes to aircraft carriers. A resource-poor nation of forty million that had to import almost all its raw materials at great hazard and was desperately short in manpower, Britain was out-producing the United States in many categories—like aircraft. America needed far more substantial production goals. A pragmatist rather than a dreamer, "the Beaver" would influence the explosive increases in American industrial output that turned FDR's "arsenal of democracy" image from metaphor to reality. By the end of the war the United States would produce more than 300,000 planes, and Henry J. Kaiser's shipyards alone would launch nearly a thousand Liberty ships, almost a freighter a day.

Confiding to his diary later, on New Year's Day, Secretary Stimson, who was not at the meeting with Beaverbrook, blamed late and laggard war production and delivery not on the industrialists but on divided priorities. As Secretary of War, the chief civilian spokesman for the military, he had to fight among rival appointees to have his voice heard by the President. Also at the President's ear were Hopkins and Harriman, agency chiefs with overlapping powers, and lobbyists for Britain and Russia. He had to weigh "loyalty to my own Army" against "loyalty to those other nations' armies" in the matter of where war output went. It was "one of the most constant, heavy strains that I have upon me."

At the same time as Beaverbrook was astonishing his listeners by challenging their mobilization targets, the British and American chiefs of staff were meeting at 2:30 in the Federal Reserve Building, planning production strategy that would soon require all of Beaverbrook's goals to be met, and more. Reporting the Beaver's concerns, Donald Nelson emphasized how "resourceful and determined" the enemy was—that we had "very little conception of the productive facilities of the Axis powers." The United States, he emphasized, had to set its sights much higher—"for the production of 45,000 tanks in 1942 against Mr. Knudsen's estimate of 30,000." Nelson also wondered why there were such production "bottlenecks" on other weapons, "the number of man-hours, machinery involved, etc." The answers were easy, but not the solutions. Industry insisted on guaranteed profits; unions insisted on requiring unwilling employees to become unionized. Dictatorial states did not have to reckon with either.

Although the cross-purposes in a free society would have a chronic impact on production, and many in industry and labor did not like the imperious Beaverbrook, his tough-minded realism may have been more significant an influence on the Arcadia conferences and the outcome of the war than either Churchill or Roosevelt.

December 30, 1941

L ITTLE BEYOND LUZON in the myriad island complex below was under enemy attack or occupation, but with MacArthur isolated, his authority, however broad, was realistically inoperative. Topside on Corregidor was largely destroyed. The Malinta Tunnel became the public center of Philippines life and government, political and military. At a small platform erected near the entrance, the ailing Manuel Quezon was sworn in for a second term as President of the commonwealth, an interim designation for the Philippines pending its scheduled full independence—assuming liberation from the Japanese—in 1946. He repeated Roosevelt's radioed promises of military assistance to repel the enemy, but his tearful anxiety for the future of his presidency was impossible to conceal. MacArthur followed with warm, unscripted words for Quezon. Then the general wept openly—either a histrionic gesture or a momentary unguarded breakdown. He looked to the skies beyond the tunnel entrance and declared, his voice shaking, "From the grim shadows of the Valley of Death, oh merciful God, preserve this noble race!"

The vague promises from Washington that help was on the way meant almost nothing. Whatever was available would be routed indirectly via Brisbane in northeastern Australia and fail to reach the Philippines. Still, the beleaguered forces isolated on

General MacArthur emerging from Malinta tunnel, Corregidor, late
December, 1941. *Courtesy MacArthur Memorial Library & Archives*

Corregidor and, very soon, Bataan looked toward the mouth of
Manila Bay and fantasized support convoys in the near distance.
Trusting in the impossible, Hattie Brantley, an army nurse on
Corregidor, recalled that "anytime anyone looked in the direction
of the Bay and did not see a convoy steaming in it was greeted
with disbelief." At night they would "go sit on the beach and
watch for the convoy that was coming. . . . It was part of the psy-
chology of survival. If you had known that you were going to be a
captive of the Japs for three and a half years, you wouldn't have
existed. You would have given up right then."

"Both forces [on luzon]," Admiral Ugaki noted from dispatches received at Kure, "have already advanced half of the whole way." They had gone much farther than that, but as defenders protected the escape route into Bataan, a Japanese regimental commander, Colonel Kawashima, was killed by rifle fire at Tarlac, halfway between Lingayen and Bataan, a rare senior casualty. Ugaki was less concerned about the Philippines, with its limited natural resources, than how to exploit the Dutch East Indies, certain to be occupied within weeks. The Germans were likely to have designs on oil and rubber and other wherewithal for its own war machine in the Indies—if Hitler could somehow lay his hands on the spoils. "It is enough for us," Ugaki thought, "to inform Germany of our determination on what to do with it," for the natural wealth certain to be seized would enable Japan "to play a leading role in establishing a new order in the world."

Activated by mutual suspicions, the unlikely Axis allies remained wary partners. By the 30th the Germans, according to Admiral Wenneker's Tokyo diary, had not received sufficient oil— only 2,655 drums—to warrant a blockade runner's hazarding homeward from Yokohama. Further, the 80,000 yen for lumber for the Japanese navy freighted riskily from Europe by the *Bhakotis* had not yet been paid. "The remaining planks and hides had still not been collected." Offshore storage was costing the Germans 3,000 yen a month. Aggrieved, Wenneker pressed a navy agent "as a matter of urgency to arrange for the cargo to be taken away. Otherwise, I would be forced to put them back on board German ships or destroy them." It was not American-style Lend-Lease.

BEFORE LIFTING ANCHOR at Ternate, reveille was held quietly on *Peary* and on shore, where some crew slept and breakfast was quickly consumed. The Dutch had brought a parting gift of three pig carcasses, for which a barbeque pit had been dug on the beach. According to the log the men "would live high on the hog," served in coconut shells, the first half-shell presented to Lieutenant W. J. Catlett, who had been reassigned rather unhappily to *Peary* at Cavite two weeks earlier after being navigator on an aircraft tender. At about noon PBY 8 and PBY 23 again splashed down near *Peary*, with dispatches and information. The crew was anxious to leave, "tired of battling the mosquitoes" and worried about the approaching enemy. As the excess camouflage was offloaded and the port screw began to turn, "Stateside fever . . . started through the ship, even talk of making a homeward bound pennant, to be flown when they entered San Diego Harbor." At 6:30 P.M. *Peary* backed into the narrow channel into the open sea and toward what was only a line on the charts—the Equator, at Longitude 126°59' East. The destroyer had only nineteen thousand gallons of fuel remaining, just enough to reach a refinery on Ambon, in the strait between the larger Indonesian islands of Buru and Seram en route to Timor (all doomed to imminent occupation) and Darwin.

"ANOTHER HARD DAY!" Franz Halder, at Hitler's headquarters in East Prussia, wrote. It was "a very difficult operational situation" all across the front, but the assault on the key Crimean port of Sevastopol, ringed by forts, was continuing. To the east, the Strait of Kerch had not yet frozen over, making resupply of nearly isolated Russian forces—a garrison of 106,000—difficult to manage. (Still, it would take until early July 1942 for the Germans to take Sevastopol, deploying the largest artillery piece ever built, the Krupp-manufactured *Gustav Gerät*, nicknamed *Big Dora*, after the *Big Bertha* of World War I. Stalin had key officers and officials evacuated by submarine. The Russian ranks fought to their deaths.) "Dramatic phone talk," Halder reported, between the Führer and von Kluge, in which Hitler—very likely screaming—refused permission to withdraw the Fourth Army. "Very serious crisis in Ninth Army, where the command must have lost its nerve for a time." By nightfall it was only "pressed back slightly," as von Kluge "appears to have asserted himself."

The *Wehrmacht* was being mauled by bitter weather as well as by the seemingly endless reserves of the Red Army, while German supply lines were overstretched and attacked, and Hitler in his dream world of *Wolfsschanze*, remote from the fronts, refused appeals to fall back to more defensible "hedgehog" lines. "Nervous tension!" General Halder closed his diary for the day.

IN PARIS the German officer who sought the trophy of *Finnegans Wake* from Sylvia Beach's shop returned. "Your copy of *Finnegans Wake* is gone from the window," he said, more angrily than before. "What did you do with it?" Miss Beach said, "I've put it away. It's for me."

"Well, you know, we're coming this afternoon to confiscate all your goods."

"Very well," she shrugged. "Do so."

"Now," he said, "will you sell *Finnegans Wake*?"

"Not at all," she said, and the officer, Miss Beach recalled, "disappeared in a rage, booming down the street. . . . I immediately had everything removed from my shop. In about two hours, there wasn't a book left in it." The concierge, Mme Allier, told her to put everything into an empty apartment on the fourth floor, and local volunteers "piled up the stairs with all those things in clothes baskets." When the Germans came they found Shakespeare and Company shuttered up. Even the shop's sign had been painted over by house painters who lived in the building, and the shelving removed. Sylvia peered out of an upstairs window but saw no Germans arrive. "They must have come and saw nothing, nothing at all. And I retired upstairs."

IN OTTAWA the PM learned from London about the increasingly grim and irreversible situation in Malaya and what it meant for Singapore. "If Malay Peninsula has been starved for the sake of Libya and Russia," he cabled Deputy Prime Minister Attlee without contrition, "no one is more responsible than I, and I would do exactly the same again." It was a cheap and unrealistic excuse for failures of planning and execution he would explain away in his war memoirs.

The PM described his two major speeches to Attlee, reported worldwide, as "extremely hard exertion" in "such an electric atmosphere." He had the added burden of Canadian relations with the Vichy puppet government in the immediate aftermath of the Gaullist takeover of Saint-Pierre and Miquelon. Rather than capitulate to the Germans, he declared to the Parliament in Ottawa, the French should have held out in their overseas empire:

> If they had done this, Italy might have been driven out of the war before the end of 1940, and France would have held her place as a nation in the councils of the Allies and at the conference table of the victors. But their generals misled them. When I

warned them that Britain would fight alone whatever they did, their generals told their Prime Minister and his divided Cabinet, "In three weeks England will have her neck wrung like a chicken." Some chicken! Some neck!

Churchill's audience exploded in laughter and applause. He had defused, at least in Canada, the issue of the two islets.

Returning to his review of contentious British-French relations, he quoted Harry Lauder's serio-comic song about the "last war":

If we all look back on the history of the past
We can tell just where we are.

Then he turned to the present—to "the period of consolidation, of combination, and of final preparation" gathering combined strength for defeating the enemies and liberating conquered peoples and territories. The next phase, he contended, would be the days of deliverance—the "terrible reckoning." With optimism belied by the facts on the ground he predicted that he was "looking forward to '43 to roll tanks off ships at different points all around Europe in countries held by the Germans, getting rifles into the hands of the people themselves, making it impossible for Germany to defend different countries she has overrun." Then, more cautiously, he added, ignoring the dates he had assigned to recovery and victory,

We must never forget that the power of the enemy, and the action of the enemy, may at every stage affect our fortunes. . . . I have not attempted to assign any time-limits to the various phases. These time-limits depend upon our exertions, upon our achievements, and on the hazardous and uncertain course of the war.

Parliament was doubly impressed that he delivered his address first in English and again in French, winning the hearts of the French Canadians. Quebecois felt closer to Paris, however jack-booted, than to London, and the curfew, they knew, had been leniently moved back for Christmas and New Year's Eve, a reward from the Germans for a compliant population.

Unexpectedly to Churchill, he had drawn the interest of an Armenian Turk who was already Ottawa's most brilliant artist in any genre. Yousuf Karsh, thirty-three, was the brother of Malak Karsh, already known for a photo of logs floating down a river that became the striking image on the Canadian one-dollar bill. Yousuf, a portrait photographer, had opened a studio in the Château Laurier Hotel, close to Parliament House, and was already known for capturing the eminent on his 8 × 10 Calumet bellows camera. A *Sunday Times* journalist would remark that "when the famous start thinking of immortality, they call for Karsh of Ottawa."

The PM was weary after his exertions, Karsh recalled, and "in no mood for portraiture and two minutes were all that he would allow me as he passed from the House of Commons chamber to an anteroom. Two niggardly minutes in which I must try to put on film a man who had already written or inspired a library of books, baffled all his biographers, filled the world with his fame, and me, on this occasion, with dread."

Churchill paused warily, "regarding my camera as he might regard the German enemy." The PM's glowering resentment at being trapped for a portrait seemed exactly what Karsh wanted to achieve, and he was satisfied; although Churchill sulkily ignored the ashtray set before him. As the cigar clamped between the PM's teeth seemed at odds with the magisterial moment, "instinctively, I removed the cigar. At this the Churchillian scowl deepened, the head was thrust forward belligerently, and the

Yousuf Karsh's iconic "bulldog" photo portrait of Winston Churchill, Ottawa, Canada, December 30, 1941. *Photograph by Yousuf Karsh, Camera Press, London*

hand placed on the hip in an attitude of anger." Karsh clicked the lens for an exposure of a tenth of a second. It took some airbrushing to make the background more luminous, the sitter less tired-looking, and his hands softened. The bulldog scowl became one of the most memorable portrait images in history.

<hr>

IN WASHINGTON at 4:05 P.M. the President opened his final press conference of the year, this time without Churchill at his side. He pointed to his nearly empty workbasket, indicating no important announcements. "Isn't that basket rather good for these days?" he remarked. Asked about a "reorganization" of civilian defense ("What about LaGuardia remaining?"), he was noncommittal about "individual personalities." Fiorello LaGuardia, however colorful as mayor of New York City, had proved unable to carry on two jobs at once and was under fire from Congress and the media. Within the week he would be left with an honorific title and effectively replaced.

"Mr. President, does the Army propose to accept the offer of Colonel Lindbergh for active service?"

"I haven't heard anything about it," said Roosevelt, cutting off that line of inquiry. The icon of the isolationist America First Committee and its platform star, Charles Lindbergh, in mid-September, appealing to a national radio audience from Des Moines, Iowa, had made the most notorious speech of his life. Attacking Roosevelt, the British, and the Jews, he deplored Nazi anti-Semitism while criticizing American Jews for urging all possible help to Britain to defeat Germany. Hitler's Germany was not America's problem. Jews were. "The greatest danger to this country," he charged, "lies in their large ownership and influence in our motion pictures, our press, our radio, and our government." Roosevelt, he declared, was a pro-war puppet of the Jews. With that the aviation hero self-destructed, and with Pearl Harbor, so did America First.*

---

*Lindbergh, who had noisily resigned his commission, would not be reinstated by the President. Quietly, several industrialist pillars of isolationism, then profiting by making armaments, employed Lindbergh, who had received the Cross of the German Eagle from Hermann Göring in 1938, as a consultant. Curmudgeonly Henry Ford brought him in to tinker with the B-24 Liberator

Other questions came up, from Lend-Lease to war budgets to making summer Daylight Saving Time year-round to conserve electric power. To many of them he parried, "You'll spoil my [State of the Union] Message to Congress if I tell you that." The minutes note "(Laughter)."

bomber at the Willow Run plant, and the ex-colonel also tested the P-47 Thunderbolt fighter for Republic Aircraft. As technical adviser to United Aircraft he even flew several missions in the Pacific. Military chiefs knew but looked the other way.

December 31, 1941
New Year's Eve

K AMPAR, A VILLAGE BELOW IPOH on the western side of Malaya, was held by survivors of the 15th Indian Brigade, who resisted stubbornly as the Japanese pushed south of the Perak River through rubber plantations and jungle. In a seized open auto, on roads so poor as to be almost nonexistent, Colonel Tsuji had left Ipoh the day before with three men, a light machine gun, and a mosquito net, essential everywhere. "Intending to share a glass of wine with the troops on the line to celebrate the New Year on the battlefield," he wrote, "we ran about fifty kilometres. Suddenly we ran into heavy shellfire. . . . It was coming from enemy guns in the mountains which constitute Malaya's spinal column, which lay across the main road. . . . Even after the position of the enemy guns was located it was very difficult to silence them owing to their concealment in the jungle." Tsuji soon came upon the captain of a company of small tanks and ordered him forward. "Yes, I understand," he said, and moved into the smoke of the barrage. "Clear of the burning shells, the tanks were soon, like snails, scrambling up the slope of the enemy's fortified position, giving great encouragement to our frontline infantry."

Behind the action, the wine camaraderie forgotten, Tsuji and his men huddled in their car under mosquito netting as it grew dark. "We were completely fagged out, and were just going off to sleep when a shellburst lifted our car off the ground. I told the driver to move a hundred metres to the rear, and we got into another position which seemed safe. We were just dozing off again when another shell landed just beside us. I said, 'Well, we better move back a bit more.' The shellfire however seemed to follow the car, and no sooner did we move to a new position than we would have to shift to another one." But the defenses were gradually giving way. The British forces had no tanks and no heavy artillery.

ON THE *Nagato* in Kure harbor, Rear Admiral Tamon Yamaguchi, commander of the Pearl Harbor strike force's Second Division, came aboard at 11:30 to brief Admiral Ugaki. Yamaguchi had aerial photographs taken from his planes showing warships capsized or crippled in the harbor as well as photos of "damages on Wake Island"—evidently prior to its occupation. He was in "very high spirits" yet displeased about the fleet's "return movement," left unexplained in Ugaki's diary. "Though it agrees with what I thought," he wrote, "it is considered better not to mention [details] here."

To Ugaki, the major question left after the two sweeps of the Pearl Harbor area had been whether a third strike should have been ordered. *Kido Butai*'s air strength was little depleted, and American sea and air pursuit was unlikely from a demoralized and badly damaged enemy that had undergone three hours of Sunday morning attacks. Admirals Ryunosuke Kusaka and Chuichi Nagumo were conferring about whether to send planes up again when the leader of the air assault, Commander Mitsuo

Fuchida, landed aboard safely. He was eager to gas up and go after what targets were missed, such as fuel tanks and repair facilities. Even a burglar, Nagumo warned, hesitates to go back for more. The victim had been rudely awakened. In evidence he noted that the flight deck officer of the carrier *Hiryu,* Commander Takahisa Amagai, had seen the results of anti-aircraft fire against second-wave planes that had barely managed to land, or fallen short, into the sea. Ambitiously, Amagai suggested, "We're not returning to Tokyo; now we're going to head for San Francisco."

Nagumo dismissed the boast as brag. He had delivered a disabling blow. Unpersuaded, Fuchida recommended going back to Oahu, but Kusaka pointed out that the aircraft carriers not located in the harbor posed a threat that could materialize at any time. (The carriers *Lexington* and *Enterprise* had been off the west delivering aircraft to Midway and Wake.) Was the little more they could do worth risking the fleet? Kusaka ordered an immediate turnabout to the northwest, as originally planned. "The attack is terminated," he said. "We are withdrawing." Shortly after one o'clock Hawaiian time (nine in the morning the next day in Japan), *Kido Butai* swung about. At Kure, learning of the decision, Admiral Yamamoto, chief architect of the operation, had mixed feelings, as would Ugaki. On his flagship *Nagato,* Yamamoto, a compulsive gambler, composed a sardonic *waka.* A classical verse form of thirty-one syllables arranged in five lines, it was adapted to his love for bridge, which he had learned when a naval attaché at the Japanese embassy in Washington in the 1920s:

What I have achieved.
Is far from a grand slam,
Let me in all modesty declare.
It is more like
A redoubled bid just made.

Whatever its success, it would prove not enough.

"We all ate noodles for New Year's Eve in the [command] cabin," Ugaki wrote, referring to the traditional delicacy for celebration. "Such customary delicacies for the new year as rice cake, sake, pine, bamboo, and Japanese apricot were well prepared. . . . I think it is too much to have such delicacies when we are in a great war. I can't help having sympathy for those men in the battlefield who have no time to celebrate the joyful new year." Still, rank had its privileges.

In Tokyo at a navy New Year's reception, Admiral Wenneker put aside friction with Japanese officialdom and, with "Party member Heck"—otherwise unidentified—handed the Vice Minister a donation of 15,000 yen raised by the embassy and the Nazi party for the naval wounded. From Berlin he received a cable authorizing German ships to cease using the "Ganges" code and to begin, with the new year, the "Himalaya" code and for the code words "Caucasus" and "Ypern" in the "Himalaya" codebook to be expunged by all vessels. Also, the special code "made up from the four strips of 'Ysop' is to be valid on a permanent basis"—which only meant until the next resetting.

⸺⸺⸺⸺

ALL ORGANIZED FORCES in Luzon that could reach Bataan were slipping through under covering fire protecting the Calumpit Bridges over the fast-flowing Pampanga River northeast of the peninsula, where the river widened into a delta and poured into Manila Bay. Aircraft supporting the Japanese 14th Army did not attack the spans, perhaps because they wanted them intact for their own use. The North Luzon Force under Wainwright was covering the withdrawals into Bataan of the South Luzon Force under Major General Albert M. Jones. His few tanks struggled up the narrow roads, and once the lead and rear tanks were disabled, the rest were useless.

Peary had dropped anchor off Ambon early in the afternoon, escorted through mine fields by a Dutch pilot who had come aboard. While *Peary* moored beside an oil dock for refueling, greeted by the Dutch, Patrol Wing Ten (the now-familiar PBY escorts), and Australian air crews and a contingent of ground troops, Bermingham granted evening liberty, warning that *Peary* would get underway early in the morning. At Ambon, seamen learned that *Heron*, an aircraft tender also evacuated from Cavite and ordered to assist the destroyer, "had passed unseen in the night. . . . On finding *Peary* had left [Ternate], she returned but had been caught by 15 bombers and torpedo planes. She had shot down one and damaged two others with her 3" AA guns, and suffered a hit on her mainmast which killed 12 men and wounded 18. . . . The pilot of the downed aircraft had refused to be rescued, and drowned." (*Heron* would limp into Ambon early the next morning.)

Liberty on tiny Ambon offered little but dry land that did not pitch and sway. Water onshore was not fit for drinking, and there was no place to go but for spare "military club facilities." Six hundred miles of ocean remained between Ambon and Australia. New Year's Eve went unrecorded.

IT WAS STILL EARLY on the 31st in Quebec. On the morning of his return journey from Canada, New Year's Eve, which like

Christmas Eve referred to the date since dawn, Churchill gave a press conference at Government House in Ottawa. "Do you think Singapore can hold on?" he was asked. "I sure do," he said with a buoyancy that belied his real estimate of the oncoming catastrophe.*

"Is Singapore the key to the whole situation from the Far East to Australia?"

"The key to the whole situation," Churchill advised, skirting the question, "is the resolute manner in which the British and American democracies are going to throw themselves into the conflict."

Asked about the situation in Yugoslavia, under the Axis heel since April but unpacified, he replied, "They are fighting with the greatest vigor and on quite a large scale, and we don't hear very much about what is going on there. Guerrilla warfare and the most frightful atrocities by the Germans and Italians, and every kind of torture." Behind the lines, he explained, "The people manage to keep the flag of freedom flying."

Responding to a question about peace feelers from the Axis, he gibed, "We have had none at all, but then I really think they must be hard pressed for materials of all kinds, and would not want to waste the paper and ink."

"How long will it take to achieve victory?"

"If we manage it well," the PM quipped, "it will take only half as long as if we manage it badly."

The special train was well into the United States and midnight was approaching when a page went through the cars announcing that the "PM" wanted all members of the press corps to

---

*The British would surrender a garrison of 85,000 to a lightly armed Japanese assault force of 30,000 on February 15, 1942. It would be the worst defeat under the Union Jack since Yorktown in 1781.

join him in the dining car. As they assembled, Churchill came in and called for drinks all around. When everyone had a whiskey or the equivalent, the Prime Minister raised his glass of Johnnie Walker, Turner Catledge of the *New York Times* recalled, and offered a toast to the Americans. "Then we Americans drank to the British, then everyone drank to Churchill. He responded by leading the singing of 'Auld Lang Syne.' When he had finished the first verse, he launched into a jazzed up version, grabbed a hand on either side, and led in a ring-around-the-rosy jig."

"AGAIN AN ARDUOUS DAY!" General Halder wrote, using language like "no defensive success." New assaults in the center were "suspended" and "heavy attacks" were "repulsed." On the frozen Lake Ladoga front in the north, near isolated Leningrad, "disagreeable attacks" continued to keep the Germans at least ten miles away. Thousands in Leningrad still died daily of starvation. In the south the front was "generally quiet"—perhaps a break in the action as the old year waned. On New Year's Eve at *Wolfsschanze*, Hitler marked the occasion with his new phonograph, a Christmas present from his staff, blurring out the gloomy news with his favorite music—recordings of Richard Wagner and Richard Strauss. Stopping the music intermittently to telephone orders to hold fast, which he barked to commanders in the East, he could hear headquarters personnel waxing merrier and merrier on whatever alcohol was available. At the frozen front von Kluge ("at the end of his wits," according to Halder) listened by phone to a three-hour tirade from Hitler on holding the line: What was needed was "a triumph of the will." In the end he grudgingly permitted tactical withdrawals, "step by step," to protect communications.

At midnight the Führer summoned his two secretaries, Christa Schroeder and Gerda Daranowski, for tea, and over his cup he fell asleep as his senior staff waited in a hallway to offer insincere greetings for the new year. Realizing the realities, Christa slipped back to her room to weep, then went off to the officers' mess, where sea-chanties were being sung with drunken buoyancy.

"FRENCHMEN!" Marshal Pétain crowed on Vichy radio as the new year approached, and as if the world were flat, "War has now spread to all corners of the earth. The Continent is in flames, but France remains outside the conflict." He hoped that in 1942 Germany and France would achieve a rapprochement that would preserve French honor, and he condemned the unceasing internal disorder, which he blamed on individual selfishness, class hatred, and the unfortunate existence of occupied and unoccupied zones. "The new order"—a term obviously borrowed from Hitler— "which is about to assume its place cannot be founded on anything but a severe internal order, one which demands from all the same discipline founded on the primacy of labor, the hierarchy of values, a sense of responsibility, respect for justice, and mutual confidence."

Then came his plea for the future. "Frenchmen! If the government which has inherited the legacy of defeat cannot always obtain your support, its acts, nevertheless, will continue French history. Its text will be written into the textbooks of your children. Strive that those pages remain written in honor and that those who come after you will have no reason to blush, either for the nation or for its leaders."

NEW YEAR'S EVE DINNER at the White House was much less
liquid than Churchill's presence would have made it. Some
perennial Roosevelt friends were present as well as Marthe and
Olav of Norway. It was far from festive at the house in
Somerville, Massachusetts, where Marguerite LeHand, FDR's
secretary and confidant since 1923, when she was twenty-five,
but now feeble from a stroke, lived with her sister. From 1925
through 1928 Roosevelt had spent 116 postpolio weeks in reha-
bilitation away from home, trying to regain some use of his limbs.
Eleanor was with him for four of those difficult weeks, Missy Le-
Hand for 110. She had a bedroom at Hyde Park and also lived
with the Roosevelts at the executive mansion in Albany and at
the White House. The President had visited her when she was
first hospitalized, but each time she became agitated and close to
hysteria. He stopped returning.

The next day, Ann Rochon wrote to FDR, Missy

> started crying New Year's Eve about 11:30 and we couldn't stop
> her. And then she had a heart spell and kept calling "F.D., come.
> Please come. Oh F.D." It really was the saddest thing I ever hope
> to see, we were all crying, she was very depressed all through the
> Holidays and that was the climax. She was expecting you to call
> Christmas Day and when we sat down to dinner her eyes filled
> with tears and she said "A toast to the President's health" and
> there again in the middle of dinner—another toast to you. She
> loves your gift and kept saying sweet, lovely, beautiful, I love it.
> She watches for the postman every trip. . . . She worries about
> you all the time.

Very likely Missy did not know that FDR, despite his distancing, personally paid every expense of her care and had amended his will, authorizing half the income from his estate (the other half designated for Eleanor) "for the account of my friend Marguerite LeHand" to cover "medical care and treatment during her lifetime." After she died in mid-1944 he would order a navy transport named for her, sending a message on its launching "in the hope that a craft which bears so honored a name will make a safe journey and will always find a peaceful harbor."

NEW YEAR'S EVE NATIONWIDE was not more muted than in previous years. Although celebratory noisemakers largely made in Japan were used with some embarrassment by partygoers who read labels, few did, and shortages had not yet occurred in food and drink. The only predictable shortage would be in rubber tires, about which the announcement was made by the Office of Price Administration that only 356,974 would be available for civilian use, two-thirds of the tires for buses and trucks. Sales of new cars and trucks were frozen until January 15, when a rationing system would be in place, and civilian vehicle production halted for the duration of the war.

Such auguries of further belt tightening meant little as the clock ticked the old year away. Under heavy skies that threatened rain, and signs pointing the path to air raid shelters that read, IN CASE OF ALARM, LEAVE TIMES SQUARE. WALK. DO NOT RUN, the neon glare of Broadway belied wartime, as did the gaiety of party horns and bells. "Tremendous waves of sound washed against the midtown towers when the traditional lighted ball slid down the *New York Times* flagpole at midnight and the lighted legend

'1942' broke bright against the murky sky." A half-million revelers filled Times Square, and another half-million who could not squeeze through crowded into streets nearby. Standing under loudspeakers in Father Duffy Square and surrounded by soldiers and policemen, Lucy Monroe, identified with the National Anthem as Kate Smith was with "God Bless America," sang "The Star-Spangled Banner," broadcast across the country, where the time zones were still marking the outgoing year.

"If there was uneasiness over the possibility of Axis bombs falling into Times Square," the *Times* reported, "you could not read it in the celebrants' faces." Despite Pearl Harbor and the reality of world war, it had not yet reached very far into the American psyche. Its reality occurred in such places as Salinas, California, where two young Japanese revelers, Teiji Fatamese and Iwau Taka, American in everything but ethnicity, were shot by other Americans who happened to be Filipinos.

On the coast itself, at San Francisco, hundreds of wounded soldiers and sailors evacuated from Oahu once the ocean passage appeared safe reached the Golden Gate. Surfaced Japanese subs had aimlessly shelled Kauai, Hawaii, and Maui, doing little damage but announcing their presence to inhibit sea activity. "Fix us up quick," one G.I. reportedly called out from his stretcher. "We want to get back."

January 1, 1942
New Year's Day

NEW YEAR'S DAY in Japan was X + 24. More aerial photos of the Pearl Harbor attacks were prominently published in newspapers from Sapporo to Kagoshima. "The people," according to Admiral Ugaki, "seemed to be delighted with them as the best of presents." Berlin radio broadcast a report from Tokyo that Emperor Hirohito spent the day "very quietly. In order to demonstrate his close union with his armed forces he had beef, pineapple and other tropical fruits for his dinner, the usual fare of Japanese soldiers fighting in Southeastern Asia." In reality, the Emperor's ordinary troops in Malaya, Hong Kong, the Indies, and the Philippines had little but rice.

At Kure the New Year's ceremony on the *Nagato*, like that on most warships, involved a "salute to the emperor's portrait, drinking the toast, and picture-taking." Ugaki hoped that the "epochal expansion of the nation"—the "first stage of the war" that had to be followed by consolidation of the gains—would be over by the end of March. He wondered what would come next. "Shall we be dragged into war with the Soviet Union, owing to a rash and thoughtless act of the army? Or will the United States and the United Kingdom recover their strength sufficiently to fight a great decisive battle in the Pacific?" The idea of a decisive naval engagement in the sea approaches to Japan had dominated Japanese and American strategic thinking since the early 1920s. It reflected the age of heavy armaments aboard battleship fortresses, predating the floating airfields that would turn oceanic war in 1942 and after into carrier-based encounters, during which crews on the decks of warships would never see the enemy, their firepower almost entirely to ward off attacks from the air.

The admiral's news from Malaya was that the southward advance toward Singapore was continuing and the air base at Kuantan, on the east coast, occupied. It was useless to the British anyway. The only planes they had were obsolete Brewster Buffaloes, now mostly debris. He also learned that submarine I-3 had sighted an enemy carrier with two cruisers one hundred miles from Oahu. It was the *Enterprise*, which had made its second return to port since the attack on Pearl Harbor. The *Enterprise* would be crucial to the great all-out battle Ugaki had predicted, for battleships would be of far less consequence than flat-tops. "Is it merely a patrol in the near sea?" he wondered. "Or will there be an air-raid to avenge our raid on Midway?" He felt that "the Task Force now making preparations at Kure [for the Indies] should be readied for immediate action as a precaution." In early June the fleet would indeed see more action—climactic action—near Midway.

A press headline in the United States reported, "MacArthur Unites His Line for Crucial Stand," suggesting that he would fight to hold Manila. The imminent "major battle" was suggested by "advices sent by General Douglas MacArthur" to Washington, but his troops had already evacuated Manila, and the capital was undefended. Asked by newsmen, Secretary Stimson said that he had "not ordered General MacArthur to leave Manila" and described his conduct of defensive operations as "masterful." Then he returned to reality. "I am perfectly confident," he said, "that we will defeat them in the end, but we cannot do it by looking through rose-colored spectacles."

The last possible crossings over the Calumpit bridges into Bataan were made just before dawn. The 12,000 Americans included one nearly complete regiment, the 31st Infantry. The Filipinos numbered about 66,000, seven small American-officered divisions, most of them more a gendarmerie learning on the job. Overseeing the withdrawal and among the last to slip in were Major General Jonathan Wainwright and his deputies, Major General Edward King, his artillery chief, and Major General Albert Jones. The bridges, now under fire, were blown up at 6:15 A.M. by a platoon of Philippine Scout engineers. The Japanese were five hundred yards away. Their artillery and aircraft pounded the forward Bataan line, which would hold for only a week. When several bombs failed to explode, curious soldiers crept out to disassemble them. Some turned out to have concrete linings intended to break up as the dynamite exploded, to scatter as shrapnel. Others contained balls of lead foil, razor blades, and parts of old automobiles and sewing machines. Why such primitive devices were being used by the well-equipped Japanese defied explanation.

General Homma's advance elements were already in Manila. Under the Open City declaration, Jorge B. Vargas, President Quezon's former executive secretary and mayor of Manila only since the previous day, on Quezon's parting instructions on December 24 had ordered the police disarmed and began pre-entry negotiations with the enemy. Vargas would become the chairman of a puppet Philippine Executive Commission. Because Homma wanted to occupy a reasonably intact city, he did not encourage his forces to rush in and rape, plunder, and torch. He knew what barbarism out-of-control forces had been employed in China. Many of his troops had been seasoned there.

From his San Fernando headquarters, retained for the reduction of Bataan, Homma ordered one regiment, the 28th Infantry, to administer the occupation. With them came the Kempei-Tai, the dread secret police. Taking over the once-exclusive Jai-Alai Club, the Kempei-Tai began preparing billboard proclamations declaring that they came "not as enemies but as liberators" and setting forth the regulations under which Filipinos were to live. Troops began rounding up Allied nationals for internment in the buildings of Santo Tomas University and setting up a government facade for Vargas in the building vacated by the American High Commissioner. The Japanese came, according to a Philippine history, with bales of already-printed, and required, occupation money, "backed by nothing and pegged to nothing" but put into circulation for the "value printed on its face."

PEARY was steaming toward Port Darwin, with two of the RAAF Lockheed Hudsons that had attacked the destroyer earlier now flying escort from Ambon, flashing, "Goodo, Yank. God's speed!" *Peary* flashed back in radio silence, "Happy landing. Splice the main brace for us tonight." A cheer went up when the crew learned by radio that *Gold Star,* with its San Miguel beer and Scotch whiskey, had made it to Port Darwin. Squalls of warm tropical rain and poor visibility slowed the destroyer from twenty-two knots to five. It would anchor the next day beside five other American ships to operate out of Darwin, most of them fated for trouble by air and sea. On January 6 John Bermingham of the *Peary* would be promoted to Lieutenant Commander, a rank he held for only six more weeks, for on February 19, 1942, Australia experienced its own Pearl Harbor. One hundred and eighty-eight Japanese planes, from the very attack force that had raided Oahu and then returned home to Kure, blanketed Darwin. Dive bombers targeted *Peary*. The fourth of five bombs which hit the ship set off the forward ammunition magazines; another penetrated the after engine room. Two of *Peary*'s machine guns were still firing as the ship went down, stern first, taking with her eighty-one men, including five of its six officers. The survivor was W. J. Catlett, hospitalized in Darwin with malaria.

Late in 1944 the widow of *Peary*'s captain presided at the launching of the destroyer escort *John M. Bermingham*.

IN VICHY, in a New Year's radio address to his rump of France, Maréchal Pétain pleaded with Germany to relax its armistice terms—an "attenuation of status." Restoration of "dignity," he argued, would lead to a "rapprochement" between the nations, and disillusioned "deserters" among public servants might return to their duties. Hitler was too preoccupied to show any interest. From his East Prussian headquarters he issued a proclamation to the German people that was unusual in that it used a proper noun he employed about as often as he referred to Christmas. "Let us ask the Lord," he appealed, "to allow the new year 1942 to bring a decision for the salvation of our *Volk*." In a supplementary Order of the Day to the military he repeated the entreaty:

Soldiers!

Now the year 1941 lies behind us! It was a year of most difficult decisions and extremely bloody battles. However it will enter history as the year of the greatest victories of all time. . . . In the year 1942, after all the preparations that have been made, we will engage the enemy of mankind anew and do battle . . . as long as it takes. . . .

Europe cannot and will not tear itself to pieces forever, so that a bunch of Anglo-American and Jewish conspirators can find satisfaction, in their business machinations, in the dissatisfaction of the people.

It is my hope that the blood that is spilled in this war will be the last in Europe for generations. May the Lord help us with this in the new year.

Adolf Hitler

In London General Brooke also invoked the Almighty. After a chiefs of staff meeting in the morning and a Cabinet meeting that he attended as COS at noon for Anthony Eden's report on Russia, Brooke turned to his diary. He had no idea yet when Churchill would return. "I pray God," Brooke wrote, "that He may give me sufficient strength to devote the energy and drive it may require. Difficult times with the PM I see clearly ahead of me and there again I pray God to help me by giving me guidance on how to handle the difficult situations which are certain to confront me."

Eden's mission to Moscow had failed. Stalin wanted no restrictions on war materiel supplied, whatever the struggle to get it past the *Kriegsmarine* in the Arctic or by any other means. Lend-Lease was neither lend nor lease. His suspicions of the West would only be mollified, he had insisted, by recognition by Britain and the United States of intended Russian frontiers—land grabs—as they existed at the moment of Hitler's invasion on June 21, 1941. He already knew there was no chance of Roosevelt's agreement or that of the American Congress. American and British military presence in Russia, even to ferry Lend-Lease aircraft across the border, would be almost nil. The Cold War was already coexisting with the hot war against a different adversary, and it would continue long past Stalin's personal rule.

As THE *Regnbue* approached closer to the American shoreline, turning to steam around Florida, the crew was permitted to use the radio receiving set in the chief officer's cabin. Liebling managed to tune into Miami, where the local announcer noted with pride that there was no frost–the temperature had not dropped below 37 degrees. Seeking war news, Liebling dialed another station and heard another announcer report, "The slant-eyed specialists in treachery continue their advance toward Singapore." Immediately after came a commercial for "creamy Sweetheart Soap."

ON NEW YEAR'S MORNING in Washington, a gray, rainy Thursday, a procession of automobiles left the White House for Virginia, crossing the Potomac to 118 N. Washington Street, Alexandria, the site of fashionable red-brick Christ Church. Built in the colonial style from 1767 to 1773, it had known several wars much too closely. In its churchyard were buried, in a mass grave, thirty-four Confederate prisoners of war who had died in nearby Federal camps. Several days in advance Secret Service agents had scrutinized the building inside and out, talked with the rector, and explained that only 250 certified parishioners could be permitted at the morning service. Eight young men of the parish were charged with the formal notifications, and early on the morning of January 1 they divided up the approved list and began knocking at doors and ringing bells. Householders barely to bed after a long New Year's Eve rubbed their eyes and learned of the special services at Christ Church at eleven.

Prime Minister Churchill and President Roosevelt greeting the daughter of the pastor of Christ Church, Alexandria, VA, on New Year's Day, 1942. *Franklin D. Roosevelt Presidential Library*

Some had suspected as much because gossip at parties the night before had spread the word that the Secret Service had examined the church—which meant only one thing. Yet no one then knew who would be permitted to attend. To be excluded at the door risked social embarrassment.

On braces only visible as the straps fitted under his shoes, the President entered the church on the arm of Major General "Pa" Watson. Churchill was accompanied by Lord and Lady Halifax, the ambassador towering over the PM. The Roosevelts, with Churchill, were seated in George Washington's pew at the front.

Parishioners sang "God of Our Fathers" and "The Battle Hymn of the Republic," after which the rector, the Reverend Edward Randolph Welles, delivered a militant sermon and read Washington's Prayer for the United States, written for the day of his inauguration, April 30, 1789. "Almighty God," it began, "We make our earnest prayer that Thou will keep the United States in Thy protection, that Thou will incline the hearts of the citizens to cultivate a spirit of subordination and obedience to government, and entertain a brotherly affection and love for one another and for their fellow citizens. . . ." Mrs. Roosevelt slipped her husband cash for the collection plate. "When these little things are taken care of by others as a rule," she would recall, "it is easy always to expect them to be arranged."

Mount Vernon was several miles up the Potomac, via the Memorial Highway built in 1932 to mark the bicentennial of the first president. Leaving church, his attendance something of a record for Churchill, who had endured divine services twice in a week, the presidential party proceeded to George Washington's home. His steel-barred tomb was unlocked for the occasion. The persistent rain had become heavy, but Roosevelt was helped out of his car and stood under a broad umbrella. Accompanied by Mrs. Roosevelt, the PM placed a wreath of red-brown chrysanthemums and blue iris, bound with red, white, and blue ribbons.

Newsmen clustered about Churchill, hoping for a remark that would go into their papers and then into the history books. "A very wet day," said Churchill to Eleanor.

"Yes it is, isn't it?" said the First Lady. In the red brick mansion the resident director, Charles C. Wall, opened the guest book for Roosevelt and Churchill to sign, raindrops from their clothes falling on the page as they did.

At lunch at the White House Eleanor had her young friend Joseph Lash seated next to Churchill. "I was too awe-struck to open my mouth," Lash wrote, but the PM was his voluble usual self. Up to date on the news, he told Lash, "Hitler had sounded awfully anxious in his New Year's message, even invoking Almighty God. But we have a presumption on the Deity."

VALERY GROSSMAN, a correspondent for the Soviet Army newspaper *Red Star*, wrote to his wife, Lyusenka, "Well, we've celebrated the new year: you in Chistopol [far to the east of Moscow], I at the front. . . . The horizon is clearing for us. There is a feeling of confidence and strength in the army, and each day brings the victory closer." He passed on snippets given to him by political commissars who wanted the remarks, however unreliable Grossman felt they might be, published to boost morale. One, allegedly from a German soldier's letter home, found on his body, was, as translated, "Don't worry and don't be sad. Because the sooner I'll be under the earth the more suffering I will spare myself."

The "Joint Declaration of War Aims" that Secretary Hull had been drafting since December 14 was signed ceremonially at the White House later on New Year's Day. It had not been easy to fashion and even less easy to obtain signatures. Churchill had refused to permit India to be a signatory, as he intended the jewel in the Crown to be a colony forever, but Lord Halifax, a former Viceroy of India, objected strenuously to Churchill and the War Cabinet and urged that the "mistake" be reconsidered. Hopkins advised the President that it was "up to the British to decide . . . although for the life of me I don't understand why they don't include [India]." When Roosevelt penned a listing of signatories on a sheet of White House stationery, India appeared among the twenty-six nations with Canada, Australia, and New Zealand, separated alphabetically by the President from the United Kingdom of Great Britain and Northern Ireland. Eden and Churchill had wanted them grouped together under Britain as a claim of continuing dependency. It seemed a bleak moment to proclaim the birth of the "United Nations," yet the nations needed the up-lifting concept.

Stalin had bridled at all the Four Freedoms outlined in the Atlantic Charter of August 1941 but especially at "freedom of re-ligion." On December 27, when Roosevelt met with Litvinov and changed the wording to "religious freedom," the President ex-pected difficulties with phraseology but told the ambassador to send it to Moscow "for comment," which surprisingly came back in two days. Stalin was ready to sign on, realizing that he could ignore any commitment. Besides, as a deputy in Moscow ex-plained Section 124 of the Soviet Constitution, "Freedom for any religion presupposes that the religion, church or community will not be used for the overthrow of the existing authority. . . ." Fur-ther, Stalin needed Lend-Lease war materiel.

"Associated Powers" had become, in the revised document for signatures, "United Nations." The long literary memory of the Prime Minister, who reluctantly accepted the order of signing, had recalled lines from Lord Byron's travel narrative *Childe Harold's Pilgrimage* from a canto published in 1816:

Here, where the sword united nations drew,
Our countrymen were warring on that day!

At dinner in the White House, the President turned to do-mestic matters, raising a surprising trial balloon. Perhaps Wen-dell Willkie, his losing Republican adversary in the 1940 third-term election, whom he had grown to admire, might be of-fered an appointment as director of industrial mobilization. As his secretaries of war and navy were distinguished Republicans, it would be another dramatic gesture beyond party labels. Always to the left of her husband, Eleanor voiced misgivings about offering Willkie too much power. Harry Hopkins suggested that because Fiorello LaGuardia had proven unable to handle civil defense on top of the New York mayoralty, it would be a good fit for Willkie. Eleanor threw up her hands in mock horror. Willkie would be offered neither post. The President would look for a nonpartisan appointee.

A new year had begun. A long war beckoned. Slow to prepare, although a sluggish Congress had its plethora of warnings, America was far from ready to fight across two oceans. At Pearl Harbor the fires were out, but vestiges of smoke still rose.

Sources

The annotated minutes of the "Arcadia" conference in Washington, December 1941–January 1942 have been published in full as *Foreign Relations of the United States: The Conferences at Washington, 1941–1942, and Casablanca, 1943* (Washington, DC: US Government Printing Office, 1968). FDR's press conference texts are drawn from the 1941 volume of *Complete Presidential Press Conferences of Franklin D. Roosevelt* (New York: Da Capo Press, 1972). Press account sources are cited in the text. Drawn from them is *One Christmas in Washington: The Secret Meeting between Roosevelt and Churchill That Changed the World*, by David J. Bercuson and Holger H. Herwig (Woodstock, NY: Overlook Press, 2005). However, the meeting was never secret; almost from the moment that Churchill arrived in the United States. Churchill's published accounts are in his multivolume *The Second World War*, fudged and altered, as detailed by David Reynolds in *In Command of History: Churchill Fighting and Writing the Second World War* (New York: Random House, 2005).

Cabinet meetings in Churchill's absence and reports to him are in Alex Danchev and Daniel Todman, eds., *Field Marshal Lord Alanbrooke. War Diaries 1939–1945* (Berkeley: University of California Press, 2001).

What Washington was like then, aside from sources noted below or in the text, can be found in David Brinkley, *Washington Goes to War* (New York: Knopf, 1988), hereafter Brinkley; and Doris Kearns Goodwin,

No Ordinary Time (New York: Simon and Schuster, 1994), hereafter Goodwin.

En Route

Churchill's preparations for Washington, his Atlantic voyage, and his stays in Washington and Ottawa are described in many sources, notably Martin Gilbert, *Winston Churchill: Road to Victory, 1941–1945* (Boston: Houghton Mifflin, 1986), and Martin Gilbert, ed., *The Churchill War Papers, vol. 3. The Ever-Widening War, 1941* (New York: Norton, 2001); the diaries of Sir Charles Wilson (Lord Moran), *Winston Churchill: The Struggle for Survival* (Boston: Houghton Mifflin, 1966); Mary Soames, ed., *Speaking for Themselves: The Personal Letters of Winston and Clementine Churchill* (Toronto: University of Toronto Press, 1998); and Jon Meacham, *Franklin and Winston: An Intimate Portrait of an Epic Friendship* (New York: Random House, 2003). The Churchill-FDR correspondence is collected in Warren Kimball, ed., *Churchill and Roosevelt: The Complete Correspondence, I* (New York: HarperCollins, 1988).

FDR in the White House in December 1941 is detailed in Conrad Black, *Franklin Delano Roosevelt: Champion of Freedom* (New York: Public Affairs Press, 2003), and more anecdotally in Goodwin, above. For Harry Hopkins in the White House, see Robert Sherwood, *Roosevelt and Hopkins: An Intimate History* (New York: Harper, 1948).

December 22, 1941

Aside from long extracts in the press, Roosevelt's press conferences were printed in their entirety in *Complete Presidential Press Conferences of Franklin D. Roosevelt* (New York: Da Capo Press, 1972), for this period, volumes 17–18, 1941.

Ambassador Litvinov's meeting with FDR (and later meetings during the week) is described by Averell Harriman, with Elie Abel, in *Special Envoy to Churchill and Stalin 1941–1946* (New York: Random House,

1975). Intimate accounts of Churchill ensconced in the White House are from butler Alonzo Fields, *My 21 Years in the White House* (Greenwich, CT: Greenwood Press, 1961); secretary Grace Tully, *F.D.R., My Boss* (New York: Scribner, 1949); cook Henrietta Nesbitt, *White House Diary* (Garden City, NY: Doubleday, 1948); map room assistant William M. Rigdon, *White House Sailor* (Garden City, NY: Doubleday, 1962); and FDR friend and dinner guest Huybertie Hamlin (as Mrs. Charles Hamlin) in "An Old River Friend," *The New Republic,* April 15, 1946.

The Eden party's departure from Russia and later at sea is described by Oliver Harvey in John Harvey, ed., *The War Diaries of Oliver Harvey* (London: Collins, 1978). Admiral Leahy's reports from Vichy throughout are from his *I Was There* (New York: 1950). David Reynolds in chapter 16 of his *In Command of History: Churchill Writing and Fighting the Second World War* (New York: Random House, 2005) states that the PM uses "sleight of hand" in his *The Grand Alliance* volume, noting that he wrote four strategy papers on the voyage, not three, concealing his "continued complacency about Singapore," omitting significant messages from London, and fudging his texts in his favor.

The war in Malaya from the Japanese side is drawn throughout from Masanobu Tsuji, *Singapore: The Japanese Version* (New York: St. Martin's Press, 1961). Hong Kong's doomed defense is chronicled by Tim Carew in *The Fall of Hong Kong* (London: Anthony Blond, 1960). Wake Island's resistance is from Bill Sloan, *Given Up for Dead: America's Heroic Stand at Wake Island* (New York: Bantam, 2003), and Matome Ugaki, *Fading Victory. The Diary of Admiral Matome Ugaki, 1941-1945,* ed. Donald M. Goldstein and Katharine V. Dillon, trans. Masataka Chihaya (Pittsburgh, PA: University of Pittsburgh Press, 1991). Further references to Ugaki's diary are from this edition.

December 23, 1941

The return of the *Akigumo* from Pearl Harbor is recorded in *The Pearl Harbor Papers,* ed. Donald M. Goldstein and Katherine V. Dillon

(McLean, VA: Brassey's, 1993). The German navy's blockade runners, and cooperation with the Japanese, here and later, through New Year's Eve, are drawn from John W. M. Chapman, ed. and trans., *The Price of Admiralty: The War Diary of the German Naval Attaché in Japan, 1939–1943, IV: 10 September 1941–31 January 1942* (Ripe, Sussex: Saltire Press, 1989). The travails of various vessels in Admiral Hart's fleet evacuating Manila through New Year's Day 1942 are recorded in J. Daniel Mullin, ed., *Another Six Hundred: A True History in Narrative Form, on the Employment of Destroyer Division 59, and Other U.S. Asiatic Fleet Destroyers during the First 35 Days of World War II, Written by a Man about Himself and Others Who Were There* (Mt. Pleasant, SC: privately printed, 1984). Events in the Philippines from the Philippine perspective here and through January 1, 1942, are drawn from the ironically titled, given its beginnings, *Triumph in the Philippines 1941–1946, prepared by the Combat History Division, G-1 Section, Historical Bulletin, XVI* (Manila: Philippine Historical Association, 1972).

Sylvia Beach's recollection of the German officer seeking *Finnegans Wake* is from her notebook on Christmas presents, 1940–1945, in the Sylvia Beach Papers, Princeton University Library, CO 108, Box 22, Folder 6, as quoted by Charles Glass, *Americans in Paris. Life and Death under Nazi Occupation* (New York: Penguin Press, 2010).

The voyage of the *Regnbue,* through to New Year's Day, is described by A. J. Liebling in the posthumous *Just Enough Liebling* (New York: Farrar, Straus and Giroux, 2004). The removal of the founding American documents from Washington is from Brinkley, above.

December 24, 1941

MacArthur's escape from Manila to Corregidor and subsequent life on the island is described by Geoffrey Perret in *Old Soldiers Never Die* (New York: Random House, 1996); William Manchester in *American Caesar* (Boston: Little, Brown, 1978); S. Weintraub in *Fifteen Stars,* above; and Teodoro A. Agoncillo, *The Burden of Proof: The Vargas-Laurel Collaboration Case* (Manila: University of the Philippines Press for the U.P.-Jorge P. Vargas Filipiniana Research Center, 1984).

December 25, 1941

Göring at Rominten Heath is from David Irving, *Göring* (New York: Morrow, 1989). The Roosevelts' Christmas presents are described by Grace Tully in *F.D.R., My Boss,* above. The effect of Missy LeHand's absence is described in Goodwin, above. Nimitz's appointment and arrival in Hawaii is recalled by Rear Admiral T. Layton, with Roger Pineau and John Costello, in *"And I Was There"* (New York: William Morrow, 1995).General Marshall's Christmas dinner is recalled by Katherine Marshall in *Together: Annals of an Army Wife* (Atlanta, GA: Tupper and Love, 1946). For Christmas Day in Hong Kong, see Charles Barman, *Resist to the End: Hong Kong, 1941–1945* (Hong Kong: Hong Kong University Press, 2009).

December 26, 1941

Boxing Day on Malta is reported by Paul Fussell in *Wartime* (New York: Oxford University Press, 1989). General Guderian's removal from the Russian front is described by Alister Kershaw in his *Hitler 1936–1945. Nemesis* (London: Penguin Press, 2000).

Churchill's angina pectoris, kept secret for twenty-four years, was revealed by Charles Wilson (Lord Moran), above. The tale of his being discovered in the altogether after his morning bath was first related in Sherwood, above. That Churchill first denied it as lacking in dignity is suggested by Reynolds, above. Map Room accounts are from Rigdon, above. David Lilienthal's diary entry on the PM's speech is from his *The TVA Years 1939–1945* (New York: Harper & Row, 1964). Tire rationing details are from an AP dispatch in the *New York Times,* December 26, 1941.

The arrival at Fort Knox of the founding documents is from Brinkley, above.

December 27, 1941

"Operation Archery" is described in Combined Operations: Operation Archery (http://www.combinedops.com/vaagso.htm). Albert Speer's meeting with Fritz Todt is from Gitta Sereny, *Albert Speer: His Battle with Truth* (New York: Knopf, 1995). Stilwell's letter is from Barbara Tuchman, *Stilwell and the American Experience in China, 1911–1945* (New York: Macmillan, 1971). Eisenhower on his crowded days appears in a volume on his early diaries, ed. Robert Ferrell, and in the multivolume *Papers of Dwight David Eisenhower*, ed. Alfred D. Chandler and his successors (Baltimore, MD: Johns Hopkins University Press, 1970), from which all Eisenhower documentation herewith is extracted. The relocation of archives documents to Fort Knox here and later is from Brinkley, above.

December 28, 1941

Marshall's rejoinder to Churchill on handling a tank is from Weintraub, *15 Stars,* above. The saga of *Peary* and his sister vessels in the fraying Asian Fleet is, as before and after, from *Another Six-Hundred*, above. MacArthur ordering *Lepanto* gold stock from Corregidor is from Carol Petillo, *Douglas MacArthur: The Philippine Years* (Bloomington: Indiana University Press, 1981). The Eden return journey from Russia is from Harvey, above. The St. Pierre and Miquelon controversy is from the *Arcadia* papers, above.

December 29, 1941

"Operation Arthropoid" was described by Michal Burian in 2002 in "Assassination–Operation Arthropoid" (http://www.army.cz/images/id_7001_8000/7419/assassination-en.pdf); and in Ministry of Defence of the Czech Republic (http://www.army.cz/images/id_7001_8000/7419/assassination-en.pdf). The relocation of Japanese embassy personnel is described in Brinkley, above. Admiral Stark's consoling message to Admiral Kimmel is quoted in Gordon Prange, et al., in *At Dawn We Slept* (New York: Penguin, 1981). MacArthur's new life on Corregidor on the 29th and 30th is described by Geoffrey Perret in *Old Soldiers Never Die: The Life of Douglas MacArthur* (New York: Random House, 1996). Churchill's arrival in Ottawa is in Gilbert (above) and Meacham (above).

December 30, 1941

Yousuf Karsh's portrait taking of Churchill is described in Maria Tippett's *Portrait in Light and Shadow: The Life of Yousuf Karsh* (New Haven, CT: Yale University Press, 2007).

Sylvia Beach's recollection of the German officer's return to Shakespeare and Company, and her concealing her stock and closing down the shop is from an interview by Niall Sheridan with Miss Beach in *Self Portraits: Sylvia Beach,* a documentary on Radio Telefix Eireann (RTE), Dublin, 1962, as quoted in Charles Glass, *Americans in Paris,* above.

December 31, 1941

Admiral Ugaki is recorded from his diary (above). Admiral Yamamoto is quoted in S. Weintraub, *Long Day's Journey into War* (New York: Dutton, 1991, 2001). Hitler on New Year's Eve is from Kershaw, above. For Wenneker and Halder, see above.

Turner Catledge reports from Churchill's returning train in *My Life and the Times* (Evanston, NY: Harper & Row, 1971). Lucy Monroe singing the National Anthem and Pétain's "Frenchmen!" radio address are in William K. Klingmann, *1941: Our Lives in a World on the Edge* (New York: Harper & Row, 1981).

January 1, 1942

Vassily Grossman's letter to his wife from the Russian front is from Antony Beevor and Luba Vinogradova, eds. and trans., *A Writer at War: Vassily Grossman with the Red Army, 1941–1945* (New York: Pantheon, 2005). Anne Rochon's letter to FDR about Missy LeHand is quoted in endnotes to Goodwin, above.

Acknowledgments

Archival and institutional acknowledgments are cited in the Source Notes and in illustrations' captions. I am further indebted for information and for good offices to Jason Alt, Jonathan, Crowe, Robert C. Doyle, William H. Duncan, Aviva Erlich, Charles E. Green, Robert Guinsler, Paul M. Kennedy, Elizabeth Kerr, Kay Li, Lannie Leggera, Michael Lipschutz, Christine E. Marra, Phoebe Mont, J. Daniel Mullin, AnnaLee Pauls, Michel Pharand, Bob Pigeon, Ben Prinmer, Mark Renovich, Richard Swain, Gabriel Swift, Lisa Tenaglie, Gregory J. W. Urwin, Rodelle Weintraub, Richard E. Winslow III, and James Zobel.

Index